UNCOMFORTABLE
INCLUSION

UNCOMFORTABLE INCLUSION

HOW TO BUILD A CULTURE OF HIGH PERFORMANCE IN LIFE AND WORK

JOE FERREIRA

ForbesBooks

Published by ForbesBooks, Charleston, South Carolina.
Member of Advantage Media Group.

ForbesBooks is a registered trademark, and the ForbesBooks colophon is a trademark of Forbes Media, LLC.

Printed in the United States of America.

10 9 8 7 6 5 4 3 2 1

ISBN: 978-1-95086-336-5
LCCN: 2020924060

Cover design by David Taylor.
Layout design by George Stevens.

This custom publication is intended to provide accurate information and the opinions of the author in regard to the subject matter covered. It is sold with the understanding that the publisher, Advantage|ForbesBooks, is not engaged in rendering legal, financial, or professional services of any kind. If legal advice or other expert assistance is required, the reader is advised to seek the services of a competent professional.

Advantage Media Group is proud to be a part of the Tree Neutral® program. Tree Neutral offsets the number of trees consumed in the production and printing of this book by taking proactive steps such as planting trees in direct proportion to the number of trees used to print books. To learn more about Tree Neutral, please visit **www.treeneutral.com**.

Since 1917, Forbes has remained steadfast in its mission to serve as the defining voice of entrepreneurial capitalism. ForbesBooks, launched in 2016 through a partnership with Advantage Media Group, furthers that aim by helping business and thought leaders bring their stories, passion, and knowledge to the forefront in custom books. Opinions expressed by ForbesBooks authors are their own. To be considered for publication, please visit **www.forbesbooks.com**.

To my parents, Jose and Oliva: Your strength, courage, and love for your children is an inspiration. You are my heroes. I love you.

--

Aos meus pais, José e Oliva: Sua força, coragem e amor pelos seus filhos são uma inspiração. Vocês são meus heróis. Eu amo vocês.

CONTENTS

INTRODUCTION

Most of us have experience with luck, both given and earned. It is what you do with luck that determines your journey, your failures, and your successes.

How I chose to overcome obstacles throughout my life, starting in high school, made all the difference to my life, career, and professional successes. Each time I overcame one hurdle, it helped me build and strengthen a foundation that enabled me to reach for and overcome ever more substantial obstacles. I was flying high and felt able to conquer any obstacle the universe put in my path. Then I reached the great white whale of an obstacle: a business with an abysmal culture, created by years of what I concluded was appalling mismanagement, months away from being shut down by no less of an entity than the US government. You don't get a much bigger obstacle than that. I saw the opportunity to join and lead that organization as its CEO as profound good luck.

It wasn't luck that enabled me to turn that entity around. I had to draw upon a blueprint of proven processes born of a lifetime of overcoming obstacles—some (most!) self-created—to build and motivate a rudderless and demoralized team into driving the success of the business. The Nevada Donor Network (NDN), an organ procurement organization (OPO), is now—and continues to be—an internationally recognized world leader in its space for several (seven, as of 2020) years running, a recognition we started earning the year after I became CEO.

The lessons I learned and applied in creating that success were not all self-created. I acquired them through exposure to the stories, experience, and guidance of similarly remarkable turnarounds.

That's the impetus for this book, a way to pay it forward—starting with the lessons I learned from my parents and subsequently from mentors and colleagues with whom it has been my pleasure and benefit to work with over the years.

BRAZILIAN BLOOD

I was born into a loving family to parents who are superlative role models for creating your luck.

My father, Jose, trained as a doctor in Brazil. My mother, Oliva, a teacher in Brazil, left there to join my father in the United States, where she ran, and continues to run, his practice.

My parents made a point of bringing their four kids in the family back "home" to Brazil every summer. We spent that time in the remote region of Januária, playing outdoors with other kids who didn't have a fraction of the material items or societal resources to support their educational and eventual professional growth that my siblings and I did.

Ever since I was old enough to understand the hard work it took for my parents to successfully navigate their way out of an area with minimal educational and professional support—an incredible lesson in overcoming obstacles—I recognized and honored their success.

Despite (or perhaps because of) being a comfortable, typical American teenager, I had obstacles of my own to overcome. A dismal high school performance, made worse by bullying and my moody attitude, made it hard for me to graduate on time. In fact, I had to take summer school my senior year of high school—the teachers there were that desperate to not have me back for another year!—

before I could get into college.

My parents' hard-work ethic had been instilled, if not activated, in me at an early age. When I finally focused on goals that I wanted for myself, a lifelong process of finding and implementing solutions to achieve success began.

WHEN I FINALLY FOCUSED ON GOALS THAT I WANTED FOR MYSELF, A LIFELONG PROCESS OF FINDING AND IMPLEMENTING SOLUTIONS TO ACHIEVE SUCCESS BEGAN.

The very first goal I established and worked hard to achieve was getting into the University of Miami. I spent a year at a local community college getting average grades before I got in. Then I had trouble maintaining a decent GPA, a situation I was able to resolve and overcome, but not before it impacted my overall college GPA. That overall GPA got me three rejections in a row—another obstacle—from the premier MBA program I wanted to attend.

Eventually, I figured out how to perform superlatively in academia and then in business. In my professional realm, I relished helping others learn how to perform superlatively as well. That's easy to do when you're working with a group of inspired and passionate professionals at a well-run organization.

It's much harder when you join a toxic organization. I joined the NDN as its president and CEO two weeks after it received the industry's *first ever* threat of decertification. Talk about overcoming obstacles!

Leveraging a lifetime of personal and professional experience, I led that organization from the worst in the nation to the top-performing OPO in the world. It was not easy. There were many "two steps forward, one step back" moments.

I learned a lot about making systemic and sustainable changes from reading the success stories of other leaders. That's why I decided to write *Uncomfortable Inclusion*.

SUPERCHARGED CAREER

I spent most of my professional career working at the University of Miami's OPO, one of only fifty-eight OPOs in the United States. Only six OPOs in the United States are affiliated with larger organizations, such as a hospital system or a university; the Miami OPO, affiliated with the University of Miami, is one of those six. All OPOs are, by law, 501(c)3 nonprofit organizations, regardless of whether they are stand-alone (unaffiliated) or affiliated. My former OPO is part of the University of Miami and Jackson Memorial Hospital— the public hospital partnered with the University of Miami faculty— so I got to work with and learn from a pack of wild and wickedly smart transplant surgeons, nurses, researchers, academics, and great business leaders. There was a lot of crossover activity; often the transplant surgeons and researchers held faculty appointments at the University of Miami Medical School while working at Jackson Memorial Hospital. It created a rich and synergistic learning environment that taught me invaluable lessons critical to my career progression.

At age thirty-seven I was at the height of my professional success at the University of Miami's OPO. I loved where I was and what I was doing. I wanted to be the organization's leader, but I knew it was unlikely I'd have the opportunity to reach the top leadership position soon. That was OK; I was content to wait.

Then I was offered the chance to lead an OPO. Of course, it was the worst-performing OPO in history and the only one to receive a shutdown threat. However, with only fifty-eight OPOs in the entire United States, the chances of another similar opportunity to lead one soon were slim to none. And I was ready to lead!

I leaped at the opportunity, with due reservations about the dismal state of affairs at the NDN and the prospect of leaving Miami, where I had a supportive community of family and friends. Everything about the decision was terrifying. I would be leaving a job that I loved, where I was well respected and successful, to join an organization similar in type but entirely dissimilar in culture and success.

The blueprint created from my personal and professional experiences and lessons I learned from others was invaluable in helping turn the NDN from the worst-performing OPO in the United States to the best one in the world.

I'm excited to share these lessons with you.

STEPPING UP AND INTO IT

When I joined the Nevada Donor Network in April 2012 as its president and CEO, it had a truly terrible track record.

The NDN was under imminent threat of decertification—the only OPO ever, at the time, in the history of OPOs, to attain such a dubious distinction. That threat came from the Organ Procurement and Transplantation Network (OPTN), a federal agency under the aegis of the United States Department of Health and Human Services that oversees the organ donation and transplantation industry. The OPTN facilitates the United States' national transplant network, which was established by federal law (the National Organ Transplant Act of 1984). There's another organization you'll hear about in his book: the United Network for Organ Sharing (UNOS), a private, nonprofit organization that manages the nation's organ transplant system under contract with the OPTN. References to their joint responsibilities are written as the OPTN/UNOS. Finally, in case you were worried there weren't enough acronyms in this book, there's also the OPTN Membership and Professional Standards Committee (MPSC), which handles disciplinary actions and performance monitoring in the OPO and transplantation space.

Removal of membership in the OPTN would have meant shutting down the entire organization and the area being taken over by one of the other existing OPOs, potentially impacting the availability of healthy donor tissue and organs for a nationwide network of patients who are the beneficiaries of our mission. It was an understandable reaction to the years of abysmal mismanagement. By 2012, NDN had an entrenched culture of fear, paralysis, and failure, further exacerbated by the abrupt departure of multiple CEOs and other senior executives in a short period of time.

I even had to move my start date up by a week because the management team was disintegrating. In the time between accepting the position and my earlier-than-planned start date, the following events took place: the interim CEO abruptly quit, with no warning; the VP of clinical affairs, responsible for a substantial part of the organization, also quit with no notice; and the board of directors received an additional notification that the OPTN, having already declared the NDN a "Member Not in Good Standing," was considering passing a motion to remove the organization as a member of the OPTN, posing a risk that it would be summarily shut down by losing its CMS certification as an OPO due to this action.

And, just to make things more interesting, a significant percentage of remaining employees—up to and including one of the company's legal advisors—believed and propagated a bizarre conspiracy theory that the NDN's horrific track record of failures throughout the organization was somehow orchestrated by a "rival" OPO in a nearby state that wanted to get its hands on Nevada's organs.

It was a lot.

A famous Chinese proverb states that a journey of a thousand miles begins with a single step. As I began applying the principles and processes that enabled the NDN's remarkable turnaround, I realized that many of them stemmed from a lifetime of experiences of overcoming obstacles. All began with similar single steps that, joined together, propelled me on a metaphorical journey of a thousand miles.

Some of those steps and influences came from my parents during my teenage years. There was my academic turnaround in college and a triple-rejection obstacle I had to overcome on my path to obtaining my MBA in healthcare sector management and policy from the University of Miami's Herbert School of Business. I thrived in my career as the director of clinical operations for the Department of Surgery, Division of Organ Recovery, at the University of Miami's OPO.

All of my personal, academic, and professional experiences gave me a sense of what is possible, even when a person, situation, or organization may seem stuck or even hopeless.

Achieving success in a seemingly hopeless situation requires hard work and a committed mindset, but it does not require the reinvention of the wheel. It does not even require luck. All it requires is willingness and a mind open to learning and implementing actions that can facilitate transformative success.

FROM POINT A TO POINT B

In late 2011 I learned of the CEO opportunity at the NDN. Here was an opportunity to lead an independent OPO not affiliated with a university or hospital system. Moreover, it was an opportunity to fix a failing, flailing organization with a wholly broken corporate culture.

When I evaluated the odds, it was clear the NDN opportunity would be my best shot to lead an OPO anytime soon.

If I stayed in Miami, the best prospect I could hope for would be to become the executive director of the University of Miami's OPO, its highest leadership position. But even in the top spot at an affiliated institution, a leader doesn't have the same freedom and creative ability as the CEO of a stand-alone, nonaffiliated organization such as the NDN. The head of an affiliated OPO has five or more bosses above them. They are subject to the budget constraints of that institution, hiring freezes, and other issues that come with being part of an affiliated organization. Most importantly, the corporate culture is set by the parent institution and it is more challenging to create and influence the culture of the OPO as a single department within a very large institution. Even if the ED knows how to improve the OPO's effectiveness, approval for the resources and changes necessary to do so would require a monumental process by people who may not understand the complex ecosystem of OPOs and transplant centers.

In March of 2012, I accepted the position as president and CEO of the NDN. I gave my thirty-day notice to the University of Miami's OPO, my professional home for many years.

Then, I got a call from the board chair of the NDN. The situation had escalated, and the MPSC was threatening to shut down the NDN entirely.

There was no guarantee I'd have time to effect the changes required to rescue the NDN from its path to decertification and closure. Every single challenging experience in my life to date, I felt, had prepared me for this daunting challenge and moment.

There are plenty of opportunities for dedicated leaders to turn around failing organizations. An organization need not be on the brink of disaster for leaders to implement changes and course corrections that can improve a company's performance by investing in employees' well-being and a strong company culture.

I believe in learning from others who have walked a similar path and applying their valuable insight to create hope for employees and leaders alike.

This book isn't just for leaders who are looking to turn around a failing company. It's also for leaders whose teams and organizations could be performing better. This book will provide insight, tools, and a path that can be customized to engender greater success at your company.

I'll start by briefly sharing lessons from my personal life as I grew from a moody, underachieving adolescent to a successful student and executive leader. I'll introduce you to the NDN, detailing the specifics of an organization that was failing in every possible way, by every conceivable metric.

We'll cover the actionable solutions I initially put in place at the NDN and subsequent initiatives to address the failures and leverage the successes of those initial solutions.

Perfection is an elusive goal. At the NDN, excellence is an achievable, ongoing goal and is why we're ranked as the top-performing OPO in the world.

We want to be the absolute best in the universe at all that we can accomplish on behalf of the heroic donors, their courageous families, and those who desperately wait for the gift of life and health through organ, eye, and tissue donation. We don't rest on our laurels, despite securing recognition as the most productive OPO in the world (based on the only internationally recognized metric for organ donors and transplanted organs per million of population served) for seven years in a row.

A lot of learning and work went into crushing those international success metrics, which we strive to outperform compared to all other OPOs each year. After six years straight of doing so, we had a good object lesson on how even the healthiest organizations still have ample opportunities to fail, learned from our failures, and emerged stronger than before. We continue to learn from management experts and from our successes and failures. We stay ever focused on continuous improvement.

I look forward to sharing the lessons from our story with you in *Uncomfortable Inclusion.*

C H A P T E R   1

INCLUSIVE, HUMBLE, EMPATHETIC

In Brazil, the government will pay for your medical school, and in return, you're offered the opportunity to work for a government hospital in a region and position based on availability. In 1965, my father graduated at the top of his college and medical school. The Brazilian government offered my father the opportunity to work as the director of the government-run hospital in the rural and mostly lower-income municipality of Januária, where he met my mother. The big-city medical jobs were reserved for doctors from politically connected upbringing and wealth, which did not apply to my father. He had charted his own path without influence, from very humble means. While practicing in Januária, one experience with a critically ill man showed my father that he was never going to get the in-depth clinical experience he needed while working for the government of Brazil.

At that time, the United States, experiencing a shortage of residents and interns, began soliciting doctors from other countries. My father would listen to old English-language records during his free time. Eventually, he learned enough English to write to the American embassy in Brazil, expressing his desire to be a medical intern or resident in the United States. He excelled in the required English-proficiency exam and a medical exam and subsequently received an internship offer in Toledo, Ohio.

After my father's internship in Toledo, he began an OB-GYN residency in Detroit, Michigan. At that point, he was able to bring my mother to join him in Detroit, where my sister was born. They moved to New Haven, Connecticut, where I was born. Then, my parents saw an advertisement placed by two physicians in Alice, Texas, a tiny town near Corpus Christi, requesting an OB-GYN doctor to join their efforts. It turns out one of those doctors was from Colombia, and the other one was from Brazil. After a phone conversation with fellow Latin Americans, my father accepted the position. My mother, in addition to taking care of me and my sister, gave birth to my two younger brothers and then started running my father's office and keeping his books, something she still does to this day, along with my youngest brother, Sergio, who I greatly admire for his incredible work ethic, loyalty, and strong family values.

Initially, my parents were determined to bring their knowledge, expertise, and children back to Brazil. We moved and lived there for almost a year. But by the time they tried to relocate us to Brazil, we had all become accustomed to living in America. My parents had previously visited Miami on vacation and loved the city's vibrant Latin American culture and large Brazilian community.

Our family's final move was to Miami, Florida. Back then, a career in healthcare was a lot more lucrative than it is today. My father built up a nice nest egg, ensuring we lived in a great neighborhood and that all four kids could go to a private Baptist high school.

One of the best things my parents did for my siblings and me was to take us back to Januária every year during summer break. It was a place where the majority of the roads were dirt roads. Many people got about in ox-driven carts and just gathered in parks to have fun, without extraneous material items.

THE SIGNAL AND THE NOISE

In Januária, my uncle, Lou, owned and operated one of the few motorcycle repair shops in the region. Motorcycles were a vital mode of transportation for those who could afford them. I fell in love with working on motorcycles and motorcycles themselves.

I was an inquisitive kid who loved to experiment with tools, science, and toys. I often took gadgets apart to figure out how they worked, then put them back together to try to create other versions of appliances and toys. It drove my parents crazy. I especially liked to dissect electric motors from remote-controlled cars, and I loved video games.

During the summers, my uncle Lou would give me repair projects; I usually returned to my family smelling like gasoline and covered in grease. My favorite memories of that time are when my uncle would take me to the outskirts of town, to one of the few asphalt roads in the area. He would let me steer the motorcycle while he sat behind me, switching the gears and holding the throttle. When I was old enough to reach the gear pedal, he let me learn to drive by myself. Each time we came back to Miami, I would try to talk my parents into buying me a dirt bike. As a compromise, my father bought off-road go-karts one Christmas for the kids. Those and boats kept me busy enough between summers when I could get back to fixing and riding motorcycles with my uncle in Januária!

My parents, and the parents of my friends in Miami, were mostly successful entrepreneurs who had built thriving businesses. They were all great sources of positive examples and support for a budding entrepreneur, which I became. My parents always encouraged their children to work hard and follow their passions. They gave us chores and paid us to do those chores. I washed cars in the neighborhood, mowed lawns for one friend's father's groundskeeping business, and even picked up and delivered reusable cloth diapers for another friend's father's business.

While I never minded working hard and finding creative ways to make money, I was a lazy kid where things like school were concerned. My parents struggled with my waking up and getting ready in time to get to school (a trait that drove my father crazy, as he was the one who drove us to school). But if I was motivated to buy something or make something happen, I was unstoppable.

The year after I graduated high school, I worked parking cars as a valet at the hospital where my father delivered babies and performed critical surgeries in the OR.

AN EMPATHETIC DEBATE

I knew what I wanted to do with the money I earned as a valet: buy a motorcycle. I was crazy about motorcycles, thanks to the time I spent working with my uncle at his garage in Januária.

I wanted a motorcycle more than anything. Specifically, I wanted a Suzuki GSXR 750. This was a powerful motorcycle with a gorgeous black-and-purple zebralike pattern (it was the early '90s). One day after a shift of parking cars at the hospital, I went to the dealership and met with a salesman to price one out. He showed me the helmet and gloves that matched the bike. After some discussion, I bought the helmet and gloves on my credit card. I told the salesman that I would be back the next day to sign the purchase papers and pick up my bike. I was still living with my parents, so there was no way I would be able to do this without involving them. I went home and told them I was buying a motorcycle.

Parental excitement did not greet my news.

My mother was devastated. She cried and begged me not to go through with it, convinced I would be in danger driving a motorcycle in Miami. She even expressed to me that, in her view, buying a motorcycle in a big city was the equivalent of certain death.

At no point did my mother or father tell me I couldn't buy a motorcycle while living under their roof. They knew I was still rebellious enough that an ultimatum would drive me in the opposite direction. Instead, they treated me like an adult, including me in their thought process and concerns. This was one of the first major lessons I received specific to emotional intelligence and negotiation. My parents kept talking to me about boats. They knew I loved boats. And they pointed out that steering a boat, even at top speed, was statistically less likely to kill me than a motorcycle. We talked for hours about their concerns and the benefits of boats over motorcycles.

I didn't get the motorcycle. I stuck with boats, specifically powerboats, which also can go fast and have loud motors. In the end, it was more about my not wanting to disappoint them rather than following their parental orders, which, in retrospect, was great leadership by my parents.

Through their personal life stories, constant immersion of us kids in their community of Januária in Brazil, and use of reason with us rather than ordering us to do things, my parents served as consistent examples of humbleness and inclusivity and empathy.

I didn't realize it at the time (what teenager ever does?), but my parents' practice of being inclusive, humble, and empathetic went a long way toward helping me grow and thrive as a manager and a leader.

I credit my parents and their Brazilian heritage for making me comfortable with seeing and showing emotion—even though that's counter to society's traditional expectations of how people should act at work. Times are changing, and being empathetic in the workplace, which requires vulnerability, openness, and trust, is key to creating a productive work culture.

EMOTIONAL SUPPORT IN THE WORKPLACE

I participated in a leadership research study[1] and was quoted in a 2019 article where the author used the headline, "Collaborative male leaders are redefining masculinity and creating healthier work cultures." In the article, I shared that I thought I differed from most male CEOs because I didn't shrink from wearing my emotions on my sleeve and that I was comfortable hearing and seeing strong emotions in other people.

BEING EMPATHETIC IN THE WORKPLACE, WHICH REQUIRES VULNERABILITY, OPENNESS, AND TRUST, IS KEY TO CREATING A PRODUCTIVE WORK CULTURE.

I said that I believe my ability to connect emotionally ultimately impacts the NDN's bottom line by "creating a work environment where people can be themselves, leading them to work with more fervor."

"If I'm in a situation where somebody is going through something difficult, or we're talking about a difficult topic, or we're celebrating something," I said, "I tend to feel those emotions and don't guard myself from expressing them." I added, "I think some leaders guard themselves because they feel like they need to be this pragmatic, all-knowing, nonvulnerable guy."

"And at the end of the day," I said, "I'm asking people to strive and thrive in an extraordinary environment, and to do that, they need to do extraordinary things. They're going to feel emotions while they're doing that. And if I deny them the opportunity to be able to express those emotions or see those emotions in me, then I don't

---

1   Carol Vallone Mitchell, *Collaboration Code: How Men Lead Culture Change and Nurture Tomorrow's Leaders* (New York: Post Hill Press, January 2021).

think we reach our full potential."[2]

The ability to be humble and empathetic is key to creating an environment of inclusivity. These are all lessons I learned from my parents first.

ROCK ME LIKE A HURRICANE

My parents encouraged an entrepreneurial mindset in all their kids.

In 1992 a short-lived business enterprise taught me a few crucial lessons that I remember to this day. One is to be quick off the mark. Two is never to let a good crisis go to waste. And three is to know the capabilities of your resources.

Hurricane Andrew hit South Florida in 1992, and the entire region was crippled. In our neighborhood, giant oak trees that had once adorned the streets now littered the roads. You could only get around if you had a four-wheel drive, due to the flooding and subsequent debris.

I had a four-wheel drive, a bright-red Jeep Cherokee that my wonderful parents had bought me two years earlier when I was sixteen.

My brothers and I, along with a good friend, Ralph, who is now a successful firefighter and paramedic on a local hazardous materials team in South Florida, had ventured out to survey the damage, and we noticed people cutting up downed oak trees with chainsaws to unblock driveways and streets. We came up with the idea to try to save some of these trees, and we went door to door asking our neighbors if they would be willing to pay us to upright and brace the oaks with two-by-four wooden planks. Most people wanted to try to save the mature trees rather than cut them up, and they definitely wanted

2   Carol Vallone Mitchell, "For the Love of Men, and Those Who Work with Them," Thrive Global, September 25, 2019, https://thriveglobal.com/stories/for-the-love-of-men-and-those-who-work-with-them/.

to clear their driveways and roads, so we had several takers. Using durable airline cargo cables and sturdy boat ropes, and powered by my four-by-four Jeep Cherokee, we saved many large trees and made several hundred dollars each. We were quick off the mark to see and execute on an opportunity to benefit our neighbors, our community, and ourselves, following that famous Winston Churchill dictum, "Never let a good crisis go to waste."

Though I didn't realize it at the time, this was also my first lesson on knowing the resources upon which your business relies—specifically, what are the reasonable expectations of your resources' capabilities and limits?

After three days of uprighting huge trees, the transmission in my Jeep blew out—and my cut of the profits went to repairing my truck. The remainder of the fallen oak trees that were blocking driveways and roads were removed or pushed upright by competitors by the time my Jeep was fixed.

Knowing the capabilities of my resources (e.g., my teams, my workforce, my business partners, my board, my Jeep) and investing in them before they break down allows me to be decisive and make informed decisions about the possibilities for growth and innovation. Without this assessment, failure is imminent, but with it, success is more certain. As for never letting a good crisis go to waste, well, I've had ample opportunities to experience multiple crises during my professional career. The number and severity of crises at the NDN surpassed anything I've experienced. And I've never let a single one go to waste.

Every summer, my parents immersed us in an environment with people who didn't have a lot. That's where I first learned how important it is to relate to and be inclusive with other people, regardless of their socioeconomic status or any other skill set or personality trait that I might assume they have or should possess.

Inclusive environments are where people feel valued, not judged, and encouraged to speak their minds even if they disagree with leadership.

I was not perfectly inclusive throughout my career, especially in the early years. Over time the power of inclusivity became a hallmark of every leadership role I assumed and decision I made.

YOU ARE GOING TO FAIL

My boss, Leslie, looked me directly in the eye. "If you keep doing what you're doing, you are going to fail as a director. And you'll never ascend higher than where you are now."

As you can imagine, I wasn't happy to hear that. I wasn't inclined to listen to my boss. She had replaced my original boss and mentor, Les, with whom I had a close relationship and who had built the University of Miami's OPO from scratch. He had deep reservoirs of clinical experience and had taught me the high standards he applied to clinical management and procedures. However, his administrative strengths weren't as refined as his clinical strengths, because he was so passionate and skilled at the clinical aspects of the mission. That's why the university decided to bring in an external executive—someone from a nonmedical industry (she had worked as a lead executive and CPA for Komatsu, a heavy-equipment company) to provide strategic and administrative leadership. My clinical mentor eventually left after a year of tension to serve as an organ recovery surgical specialist at the LifeCenter Northwest OPO in Seattle, Washington.

In fact, soon after my beloved former boss and mentor had left, he recruited me to work at the Seattle OPO. At that time, my title was supervisor. The new boss recognized the depth of my clinical expertise and rerecruited me to stay at Miami's OPO and promoted me to manager. A few years after that, she promoted me to director, a position that gave me more responsibilities and direct reports and expanded my focus on interacting with the families of heroic donors.

My new boss (I still thought of her that way even after a few years) utilized my clinical expertise and often had me attend strategic and administrative meetings. Despite her recognition and support, I continued to see her experience as less relevant, and I still blamed her for the departure of my clinical mentor. And her giving me access to high-level meetings I wouldn't have participated in otherwise didn't make me more receptive to her statement that I was failing in my role as director.

My previous performance evaluations were all very complimentary. What she noticed and needed me to notice was that I wasn't getting the big picture.

As director of clinical operations, I headed the department that facilitated all clinical operations related to organ recoveries and transplants. My team of twenty-five direct reports consisted of surgical recovery coordinators, referral responders, family service coordinators, and donor management coordinators who managed the process and procedures that took place in the ICU and OR after a heroic donor's suitability and authorization status was confirmed.

Of course, I didn't appreciate my boss's feedback when I heard it. I barely even heard it. I just thought what she said—and put in my written performance evaluation—was a crappy thing to say. I felt disgruntled, deflated, and deeply unappreciated.

Didn't she see that I was killing myself at my job?

She did.

That was her point.

At the time, I was making the same mistake many up-and-coming leaders and managers make. I believed to get a job done according to the highest possible standards, I would have to do it myself and always be involved. After all, I reasoned, it would take too long to teach someone else how to do it. Even if I did show someone, I couldn't be sure they were adhering to the same level of perfection I practiced.

Right?

Wrong. So wrong.

My boss told me that trying to do everything was not helping me grow as a leader. Worse, my insistence on being involved with every donor impacted my ability to move up the career ladder and to help more people.

Even though I had a team of people whose responsibility it was to learn and perform the clinical tasks my previous boss had taught me, I knew I alone would perform them as expertly as possible. Time is always of the essence when it comes to heroic donors who are critically injured, and for beneficiaries who are on a ticking clock, desperate for lifesaving organs and tissues. Efficiency and expertise matter.

Why wouldn't we want the best person for the job—me—conducting as many of those procedures as possible? I was driving all around South Florida in the middle of the night, leading by example—I thought—doing everything my team would do. My boss, instead of recognizing and appreciating my efforts, specifically called my efforts out as career limiting and not particularly helpful.

I was so hurt and angry that it took me a while to realize she was right.

Yes, I had built up the knowledge and clinical expertise critical to this part of the heroic donor process. I gained that knowledge because someone had *taught it to me* before moving on to another role.

Oh.

Got it.

When I became a director, I hesitated and struggled with letting go of all the tasks I had mastered, partly because I thought my mastery was a critical part of my career growth. I missed the mark by not being inclusive and spending the time to train people whose jobs were to conduct these clinical procedures. In fact, they were equipped to do it even better than I could, based on their clinical and medical backgrounds and personal career paths. Yes, leading by example is important, but not when it gets in the way of developing others to their full potential. Both my current boss and my former boss taught me skills that were meant to be passed on to others so that I could continue working on myself once the process was up to someone else.

By holding on to the tasks I was doing before my promotion—insisting on conducting on-site procedures that my team was supposed to conduct—I was not doing my job as director. I was not leading or empowering my team to do the high-stakes, high-risk procedures they wanted and needed to do to strengthen my overall department's capabilities and breadth.

Eventually, I understood what she was saying, yet I *still* was resistant.

If I trained someone to perform those procedures as precisely as I was taught, it would take me three times longer than if I did it myself. I could put lines into somebody for invasive pressure monitoring and/or take the lymph nodes out for compatibility testing in less than an hour. Training someone would take three hours, and my department conducted approximately 150 of these procedures each year.

It took my boss telling me I was failing before I realized that to become the director the OPO needed, I had to empower the team and be inclusive with the knowledge that I had acquired.

I finally got over myself.

I started by training two people on how to perform procedures the way I was taught. It took a long time, it was uncomfortable, and it was tiring, not because of the people I was teaching, but because I *still* insisted on doing most procedures myself.

By teaching and allowing others to learn, grow, and flourish with new expertise, I was inclusive and gained time to grow, learn, and thrive in my new role as director of clinical operations.

My supervisor was, of course, a remarkable administrator with decades of executive experience. She practiced inclusivity by including me in as many strategic meetings as possible, where she relied upon my depth of policy and clinical expertise. Thanks to her, I served on many of the OPTN/UNOS national committees as the clinical policy expert and front-facing individual of the University of Miami's OPO. That experience proved to be incredibly useful. Working with her, I learned a tremendous number of nonclinical executive skills having to do with strategic planning, budget issues, HR issues, hiring and termination concerns, and legal considerations, all of which helped me round out my overall career skill set. Finally, guess who was one of the biggest supporters of my decision to apply for the MBA program at the University of Miami?

She was a major advocate in helping me obtain the scholarship award I eventually secured, which allowed me to attend that particular MBA program.

Thanks to her explaining how I was holding myself back, then giving me more responsibility once I had figured out how to let go, I was able to allocate my time to pursue and then obtain my MBA while holding down a full-time job. Until I did that—let go and teach others to perform procedures I had insisted on performing myself—I had zero mental headspace to spend weekend time applying and studying for an MBA. As uncomfortable as it was, her mentorship with this lesson was pivotal, and that is something I will never forget.

The incredibly valuable lesson my boss's candidness provided was the practice of uncomfortable inclusion. By listening to her feedback and adjusting my behaviors, I benefited my career, team, department, the University of Miami's OPO, and the career trajectories of everyone in my department.

A team is greater than the sum of its parts (a paraphrase of Aristotle's adage that "the whole is greater than the sum of its parts," to define synergy). That's a lesson I'd learned while captaining a boat with my siblings. But I had to relearn it as a professional. And that's usually the case. It's rare for anyone to learn a leadership lesson perfectly the first time.

TEACH A MAN TO FISH ...

As I shared earlier, my parents had done a masterful job in turning my interests from motorcycles to boats. When I was in college, my father helped me purchase a boat in lieu of a motorcycle.

I loved that boat. My siblings and I spent most of our free time on it. But *I* was the captain. My love affair with the ocean and boats started with my favorite movie of all time produced by Steven Spielberg called *The Goonies*, released in 1985. I was eleven at the time and became fascinated with pirate ships, treasure, and all the misfit characters facing difficulty as the outcasts of the Goon Docks in Astoria, Oregon, who were not the most popular kids in school. But they were one of my earliest recognitions of the enormous capabilities of a passionate and committed team.

Nonetheless, as captain, I insisted on doing everything myself. When something needed to be done that required my siblings' help, I didn't let them practice what they had learned; I ordered them to do what I knew—or thought I knew—was right.

As captain of the boat, I felt I needed to take and be in control of everything, including getting all the supplies we needed, rigging all the bait, and making sure the equipment was working.

It was exhausting.

Part of owning and captaining a boat went hand in hand with an obsession with fishing. My brothers and sister and I started entering fishing tournaments, which are usually stocked with older men and women with decades of experience in fishing competitively. My siblings and I were a team of four kids in our teens and early twenties.

Of course, my autocratic style resulted in fights with my siblings. My attitude created an unpleasant and unhelpful dynamic out there on the water—where we were supposed to be having fun during a competition—because I couldn't get over myself and let my team drive the boat or decide what kind of bait we would run that day.

One day, we were nearing the end of the contest—the time by which we had to be back at the dock and have our fish weighed. Under my rigid command, we hadn't caught anything significant. We were thinking of wrapping it up and heading back to the marina to join the tournament's after-party.

We were about twenty miles away from the dock when someone (not me) noticed circling birds and suggested we go see what was going on. It turned out there was a feeding frenzy; by skirting the edge while trolling our baits, we hooked a fish. Not just any fish—a truly gigantic fish. It was clear this fish was going to catapult us from after-party participants to significant contenders. Once we landed the fish, which took a team effort, we had less than thirty minutes to make it back to the dock and get the fish weighed. Luckily, we were in a following sea, when the tide was going in, and we had help from the waves along with help from every person on deck doing their part to make the boat go as fast as possible. I had no time to direct anyone to do anything. I focused solely on aiming the boat to the dock and holding down the throttle. My siblings were responsible for everything else. We made it with two minutes to spare thanks to my incredible brothers Sergio and Alex sprinting to the weigh station to present the fish to the tournament officials.

The officials weighed the fish: it was the heaviest fish of the day!

That was one of the first significant tournaments we won, and our beautiful trophy, sculpted and donated by a famous local artist, still holds a place of pride at my parents' home. After that experience, we began to routinely place in the top five in all the tournaments we entered. We were in my little twenty-three-foot boat with a single motor, competing against much larger boats that could go longer distances to catch big fish. Those boats and their crews were better funded, had more substantial equipment, and had far more experienced teams. However, we managed to place in the top five in most of the competitions we competed in during the many subsequent years we all fished together.

The day we caught the huge fish is when I began to really trust in my siblings' expertise and decision-making and didn't feel I needed to be in control of everything all of the time. I let them do what they wanted and knew how to do, things they all eventually did better than I did. I still was captain. But the overall success I enjoyed happened because I began trusting my crew. They had skills they were eager to practice and improve upon based on their high standards and expectations of what we could achieve together. Like the Goonies, no matter how goofy the crew was, they all had something to offer the team. When they worked together, they achieved success beyond their wildest dreams to find One-Eyed Willy's treasure to save the Goon Docks and their homes!

GETTING OUT OF THE WAY

Any team, whether it is a team of siblings on a boat in a fishing tournament, a group of medical professionals at an OPO, or an entire company, is greater than the sum of its parts. Magic happens when individuals are empowered to double down on their strengths, get out of their own way, and invest in the resources they need to improve in areas where they can get better.

> **MAGIC HAPPENS WHEN INDIVIDUALS ARE EMPOWERED TO DOUBLE DOWN ON THEIR STRENGTHS, GET OUT OF THEIR OWN WAY, AND INVEST IN THE RESOURCES THEY NEED TO IMPROVE IN AREAS WHERE THEY CAN GET BETTER.**

A team of people can achieve more than a leader when they all work together. As a manager and leader, the best thing I can do for someone is to say, "Here's how I learned how to do this. Have at it, and I have your back, and whatever else you need to keep growing and learning."

I had to learn how to get out of people's way to let them grow. First, I had to learn (and relearn, and then learn again) to get out of my own way to enable my growth as a leader of people, teams, departments, and eventually an entire organization.

I had to practice looking at long-term versus short-term benefits of how I managed.

The short-term benefit of doing everything myself is that it is done to my specifications, but if I focus on that, I'll never grow beyond doing discrete tasks. The long-term benefit of teaching others how to fish, literally and figuratively, creates a team that deeply appreciates the opportunity to learn, develop new skills, and advance their career path. It also frees up my time to focus on strategy.

This is not a one-and-done type of lesson. It never is.

I served as the director of clinical operations for seven years at the University of Miami's OPO. The preceding seven years were spent obtaining higher positions. For most of my fourteen years total at the University of Miami's OPO, I had to hire as well as manage everyone on the teams I was responsible for.

Management is different from hiring, which is a whole other kettle of fish. Over time, I learned not to exclude a potential hire because they didn't have the specific title or credentials I first thought were necessary.

Hiring well was a lesson I had to learn more than once. As the newly appointed president and CEO of the NDN, I quickly hired a few different senior leaders to fill leadership gaps. Once again, I was pretty sure I knew the right thing to do as the leader of an organization. And once again, I was wrong. I'll discuss those experiences in more detail in chapter 6 ("Building a Successful Internal Culture: Two Steps Forward, One Step Back").

My fit for the role of president and CEO of the Nevada Donor Network didn't start with the leadership skills I had honed at the University of Miami's OPO, or while getting my MBA.

Becoming the right person to turn the NDN from the worst-performing OPO in the world to the best-performing OPO in the world started with skills I learned as a result of almost failing out of high school.

TURNAROUND TEMPLATE

I went to a private Baptist school, one year behind my sister, Priscilla, a fantastic student. These days she is a successful academic recruiter with two master's degrees who speaks four languages and is the most compassionate human I know. All the teachers in high school loved her.

They didn't feel the same way about me at all.

By all accounts, I was a Goonie. I was a terrible student with a real attitude problem. I mouthed off a lot and cut class. I never did drugs or anything truly awful (that would have meant immediate expulsion as well as breaking my parents' hearts). I definitely would have been kicked out of school if there weren't four kids in my family, representing four expensive tuitions. The Baptist school wasn't going to turn that income down.

One teacher was so infuriated by my attitude that after he kicked me out of class, he shoved me up against a wall. The principal happened to be walking by at the time, so the situation didn't escalate. The teacher wasn't punished—the principal had probably thought of doing the same thing.

I failed three classes in my senior year. Normally, that would require someone to repeat the year entirely. However, I strongly suspect

I was allowed to graduate "on time" because no teacher wanted me in their classes again. I spent the summer after my senior year of high school in summer school, passing the three classes I had failed initially. I went to a local community college for my freshman year.

I had a tough time of it in high school. Being out of shape and not adhering to the strict social cues and norms of high school society made me a target for bullies. I was rebellious and didn't care for teachers telling me what to do. I didn't like how strict my school was (they didn't even allow dancing—like the town in *Footloose*), and I'd spend a lot of time hanging out with the kids at the public high school down the road. My Catholic and Brazilian parents, on the other hand, were totally comfortable with dancing and alcohol.

I was lucky in one respect—I had several great friends in high school. These guys grew up in families similar to mine, and their parents were like my own. In fact, I'd listen to their parents more than mine! My friends were hard workers and, like me, were into motorcycles and boats.

One friend, Hector, whose dad started a landscaping and groundskeeping business, now manages major assets and resources for a sovereign state in the Middle East. Another friend, Sean, whose parents built and sold a large electrical contracting company, started working early at Home Depot, rose far up the ranks, and now is a high-ranking executive at one of the few remaining successful retail clothing chains (with nearly 1,500 stores) in the United States. And my friend Joel is a command master chief over a fleet of nuclear submarines for the US Navy.

We all share similar ideals and work ethics, and we're all pretty successful in our respective fields. Our families consistently exposed us to a humble, inclusive, empathetic, and hard-work mentality that set us all on the "right" path. That path was rarely a straight one, but it was definitely the right one, given that it got us all to the places we occupy professionally today.

COLLEGE BOUND

By the time I started caring about college, my GPA was too far gone even to consider applying to the University of Miami (my dream school). It was a waste of an application fee, but I tried anyway and was rejected.

But I wasn't willing to go anywhere else.

The very first significant obstacle I had to overcome was my failure at high school. So I spent a year at a local community college, retaking basic and advanced (for high school) courses and scoring well enough to apply to the University of Miami again, which accepted me as a freshman this time.

There was barely any time for me to enjoy my admission accomplishment before I experienced my next failure: not getting good grades at the University of Miami.

Despite my newfound determination to study, I struggled and only managed a 2.3 GPA my first two years. That's because the study skills I finally improved, the ones that got me out of community college and into the University of Miami, came down to nothing more than rote memorization. And at some point, memorization was just not enough.

I knew I was working hard, so I couldn't fault myself there. I was memorizing as much as I could, but my GPA remained mediocre. I stressed about costing my parents tuition money while I was performing poorly.

LET'S GET CONCEPTUAL

One day, I was studying for a basic-level psychology class exam, and something clicked. I was reading about the common factors that motivate and drive development and success. The topic fascinated me. I understood the concept, which negated the need to try to memorize every single example mentioned by my teacher or in my textbook.

In a class of two hundred students, I got the highest grade on the subsequent exam.

Everything about how I learned changed. (This may be the only example of a "one-and-done" lesson in my life. I never went back to rote memorization for anything other than people's names and, further along in my career, unchanging clinical tasks.)

I made an appointment with my psychology professor to discuss my inexplicable great grade. I shared that I had been struggling grade-wise and asked him if he had any insight into why I had done so well on that particular exam.

He told me he had witnessed similar transformations in other students when they figured out that a previous learning style that had served them well no longer did so. That made sense; this exam was the first in which I had practiced understanding new ideas conceptually.

The professor stressed that if focusing on learning things conceptually got me high grades, then I should continue to focus on learning that way, rather than memorizing every single item cited by an instructor or textbook. By learning concepts, he pointed out, I'd be able to answer any question based on that concept, whereas trying to memorize everything by rote would only benefit me if an exam featured the same example from the textbook.

I never looked back.

Over time, I realized that another useful tool in my learning (and teaching) arsenal stemmed from storytelling. Learning concepts is more powerful than memorizing facts; thinking about concepts in the context of stories is an even more powerful tool for understanding new ideas.

> **LEARNING CONCEPTS IS MORE POWERFUL THAN MEMORIZING FACTS; THINKING ABOUT CONCEPTS IN THE CONTEXT OF STORIES IS AN EVEN MORE POWERFUL TOOL FOR UNDERSTANDING NEW IDEAS.**

Later in my life, I was invited to teach management courses to other emerging leaders at the University of Miami. Those courses had specific materials and examples, but I'd always augment them with my own experiences and stories from my career. Facts and concepts shared through the lens of stories that demonstrate "proof of concept" drove home the point of the lessons I taught. Real-life examples are always the most memorable and compelling.

During my final two years at the University of Miami, I landed on the dean's list and provost honor roll before graduating with a bachelor of science degree in microbiology and immunology. I realized I was smart enough to compete with all the other students, and I could get good grades if I put my mind to it: a perfect example of working smarter, not harder (though hard work is always crucial).

LIFE-CHANGING TIMES

After I graduated from college, I thought I would become a doctor like my father. I began studying for the MCAT while working as an orderly at the hospital where my father still practices to this day as a surgeon, delivering babies and attending to patients in the ER with

OB-GYN complications. That hospital was one of many in a specific geographic region contracted with the University of Miami's OPO, which meant the hospital would alert the OPO team if they had a potential heroic donor.

It was at that local hospital where the train of my life switched tracks—from becoming a doctor like my dad to focusing on a career in the world of organ procurement and transplantation.

Donor recovery procedures, in which a surgical team can recover viable organs and tissues from a heroic donor, are episodic and rare at smaller community hospitals. So many different variables have to be met for that type of procedure to occur that most medical professionals can go their entire career without witnessing an organ recovery. An individual must be a registered donor or someone whose family agrees to support the organ donation process. The person needs to be in relatively good health to improve the odds of the clinical viability of the organs and tissues they donate. There needs to be an absence of significant diseases, cancer, or other serious medical ailments. At small community hospitals, organ recovery cases may occur fewer than five times a year. (At larger trauma centers, the average could be closer to sixty a year.)

I worked as an OR orderly, which means, between my mopping bloody floors and prepping patients for elective procedures, rare cases like this were always episodic, never scheduled. An OR orderly prepares and sets up an OR with general-use equipment for routine procedures all the time. When an emergency requiring surgery comes in, the orderly gets a preference card that details the specific equipment needed. On the night that changed the course of my life, I was handed a preference card for such a rare event—an organ recovery procedure.

For organ recovery, an OR orderly gets a short sixty to ninety minutes to prepare a room (usually it is thirty minutes or less). There is a lot of specialized equipment designed to extend the viability of a newly recovered organ and conduct those unique surgical procedures on a heroic donor to save the lives of others.

A fifty-year-old woman had suffered a stroke, leaving her with irreversible brain and brain stem damage, and she was on a ventilator. She fit all the requirements, and her family authorized her as a heroic donor when she was declared brain dead. The OR preparations were completed and the surgical team of doctors, nurses, and technicians assembled. (You can read a detailed description of the organ recovery and transplantation process in the appendix.)

The surgical team spent a lot of time explaining what they were doing, talking through the rationale and steps of the entire process that night. These professionals on hand in the OR were personnel from the University of Miami's OPO. Doctors, nurses, and technicians who perform these rare procedures are generally very good about sharing practical knowledge to educate other medical professionals on the importance of organ, eye, and tissue donation.

The person I interacted with the most during the recovery was someone on the OPO team. He was very thorough in his explanations, talking through the logic of why they were doing things a certain way, describing solutions used for organ and tissue preservation, and discussing the time limitations around removing, transporting, and transplanting different organs and tissues.

One aspect he explained in detail had to do with keeping an organ viable by immersing it in a solution that is cold enough to preserve its viability by minimizing the impact of the low oxygen conditions in the containers used to transport them. The people who manage the viability of organs are called organ perfusionists or surgical recovery coordinators.

I was immediately captivated by the magnitude of the heroic gift and the humanitarian benefits of the process. I knew I was privileged and lucky to witness it.

The person from the OPO's organ recovery team who had answered most of my questions said, "Hey, you seem really interested in this. We have an open job for an entry-level perfusion technician. You should consider applying for it."

Organ recovery and transplant perfusionists are different than traditional heart and lung perfusionists. OPO perfusionists bring a host of solutions, supplies, and machines to preserve isolated organs as they are recovered.

I applied, hoped, and prayed I would get the job. The interview process was long and tough. Through that process I met a great friend named Mike who still works for the University of Miami OPO today. He is also a courageous firefighter and paramedic with a local fire department. I found out later that he put in a great word for me as the preferred candidate for the position, which I am eternally grateful for, as he helped set me on a new and magical path. Eventually, I was offered a job as an entry-level perfusion technician!

Initially, I intended to use that job to bolster my medical school application. I figured I'd just scrubbed in on a rare organ recovery procedure, and I was on the grounds of an OPO where I would be able to see more organ recovery procedures, and I would be at a hospital where I could sit in on transplant procedures. It's rare to have the opportunity to witness both sides of the organ recovery and transplantation process. I knew I would absorb an incredible amount of clinical knowledge that would give me an edge when applying to medical school.

I quickly found myself more captivated by my job at the OPO and less interested in going to medical school. I spoke to my father about my new passion and energy for the OPO space.

My dad told me that if I was that passionate about the OPO arena, I should consider exploring it as a career, because what it meant to be a doctor had changed in the time he had become a physician. I wanted to be a doctor because I wanted to be like my dad; I wanted to follow in his footsteps and make him proud. I was continually in awe of the lifesaving work he performed in the operating room delivering babies and in taking care of patients. My dad helped me understand that if I chose something that I was 110 percent passionate about, then it was totally OK for me not to go to medical school. He pointed out that the donation and transplantation mission of OPOs meant I could still be part of a critical care team in the hospital and beyond.

I needed that affirmation.

With the MCAT and medical school safely in my rearview mirror, I completely immersed myself in my new career. I loved every single minute of it.

ROCKETMAN

The OPO promoted me to chief perfusionist within two years. During that time, I also earned my credentials as a certified procurement transplant coordinator, or CPTC, which encompasses the entire process of donation and transplantation. Less than a year later, they promoted me to supervisor, then manager. I received five promotions in seven years, eventually securing the role of director of clinical operations for the Department of Surgery, Division of Organ Recovery, an enormous job. We were responsible for a network of more than eighty hospitals that depended on us to facilitate fast and efficient organ recovery and allocation. Our department made rapid, critical lifesaving decisions; our team management and dynamics were essential pillars that supported our ongoing growth and success while working in a premier academic and research institution.

I had found my lifelong passion and felt like the luckiest person alive. It was around this time that I discovered that I qualified for a tuition remission program as an employee of the University of Miami. It was awarded yearly to up to four individuals interested in pursuing a master's level education.

Once again, I was determined to pursue a higher level of education. This time, I specifically wanted to get an MBA with a specialization in healthcare administration and policy at the University of Miami's Herbert School of Business.

I had an incredible amount of confidence based on my career success to date, a history of making good grades during my final two years of college, and an excellent reputation at one of the most impactful medical departments at the University of Miami.

I was a shoo-in for this award, I thought when I submitted my application.

So naturally, I got rejected.

Three times.

CHAPTER 3

A MASTER'S DEGREE
IN PERSEVERANCE

While I worked at the University of Miami's OPO, its business school (renamed the Herbert School of Business in 2019) underwent remarkable and significant change.

Donna Shalala, secretary of health under Bill Clinton, had joined the University of Miami in 2001 as its president. She immediately recruited a formidable faculty to lead its healthcare business school. The University of Miami became even more highly regarded for its academics under her reign. Today its MBA program is one of the top-ranked healthcare programs in the country because of its high-caliber faculty and Secretary Shalala's accomplishments.

The executive MBA program was perfect for a busy working professional. An intensive two-year course was taught only on long weekends, which allowed students to continue working full time. Getting an MBA would open up more significant opportunities for advancement at my current organization.

My parents were extremely generous to me and my siblings, paying for our private high school, undergraduate educations, and, in some cases, graduate school. With my dad being a successful doctor and my mom a former schoolteacher, they always emphasized the importance of education to us and invested in our futures without hesitation. So you might be surprised to hear how tenaciously I pursued a full-tuition scholarship to obtain my MBA at the University of Miami. It was because of another painful, yet ultimately useful, life lesson.

While working at Miami's OPO, I had the opportunity to invest in a condominium during the burgeoning Miami Beach real estate boom. People were making lots of money buying and renting condominiums through an ingenious hotel/condominium combination.

As a child of immigrants to America, I have a unique perspective on housing and real estate. Securing housing means securing survival in most parts of the world, including the United States. The importance of having a secure and safe place to call home is a crucial contributing factor for educational and professional success. It's a lesson I partly absorbed through my parents and their friends, who obtained lovely and secure homes for their families in Miami. Through our repeated family visits to Brazil, I saw firsthand how secure housing, or lack thereof, plays an enormous role in the opportunities a person can pursue. Investing in real estate is more than just making money—it's an investment in a community and society overall that empowers people to improve their living situations for themselves, their parents, and their children.

From an early age, I understood the immense power of owning real estate. I envisioned operating a significant real estate portfolio that provided people with a safe and secure place to live that they otherwise would not be able to afford, giving them a foundation to pursue educational and professional goals. I've spent decades slowly investing in that vision.

Back in the late '90s, Miami Beach underwent a significant

change. It had been very *Miami Vice*, with lots of drugs, crime, and clubs where people went to conduct all manner of nefarious business. Then a gentleman introduced my new OPO friend Mike and me to a new mixed-type real estate opportunity in Miami Beach. Owners of a condominium/hotel hybrid could either live in their condominiums and enjoy hotel amenities or rent the condos through the hotel to visitors to Miami Beach.

I was making around $50,000 a year. Between my savings, salary, and my father's willingness to be a cosigner, I was able to invest and purchased a condominium.

From 1998 to 2000, I was riding high. The returns were phenomenal: a unit purchased for $150,000 was rapidly revalued at $250,000, equity that I could use to buy more condominiums, which I did.

My parents and one of my younger brothers saw the impressive appreciation of my real estate investments. I suggested that they consider investing with me to purchase more real estate as a vehicle that would support my parents during their retirement. My dad thought that was a good idea. He took out a considerable amount of equity in their home and handed me a check for a few hundred thousand dollars. My brother followed suit.

It was the end of 2000. My friends had been enjoying impressive financial success in the stock market, playing with margin accounts, and generally cleaning up. I decided to follow their lead, double the collective funds made up of my family's money, cash out, and put the increased proceeds into Miami real estate.

Then the dot-com bust happened.

Our collective family funds in the stock market evaporated, and my real estate holdings were all in the red. The depth of shame and sadness at losing my brother's and parents' money devastated me.

All told, I was $300,000 in debt. As the person who suggested going all-in with the stock market, I took full responsibility for paying back funds given to me by my parents and brother. In retrospect, this was a great lesson in owning responsibility entirely when things go wrong.

It was several years later when I learned of the highly competitive University of Miami MBA tuition scholarship, awarded to only four students a year out of fifteen thousand employees. I knew that executives with MBAs could secure higher salaries. A higher salary would allow me to pay back my parents and brother more quickly.

The catch was this: any money I spent toward getting an MBA was money I wasn't using to repay my family. I couldn't live with that. That's why I was determined to secure the full-tuition scholarship. It was the only way I could live with myself and get my MBA.

For someone to win the tuition remission award and get accepted to the business school at the University of Miami, they had to have a stellar work record, letters of recommendation, and a track record of academic—and if appropriate to their age, professional—accomplishments.

I thought I had it in the bag.

This was the same University of Miami where I'd landed on the dean's list and provost honor roll during my last two years as an undergrad. The University of Miami had even asked me to teach business management courses to other employees at the university based on my career at its OPO. I had been doing this for a few years by the time I started looking into getting an MBA.

University of Miami employee?

Check.

Stellar work record?

Check.

Letters of recommendation?

Check.

History of academic and professional achievements?

Check and check.

Then I applied to the MBA program and tuition scholarship.

No check.

What the hell? These people at the University of Miami knew me. I met all the requirements and then some. Surely my college GPA was readily excusable when you considered my academic accomplishments in the last two years of undergrad and all that I had accomplished in my professional career.

Nope!

My first rejection was not for the tuition scholarship award. I wasn't eligible for it because the MBA program hadn't accepted me, period. That was because of my poor performance during my first two years in undergraduate studies at the school and my overall 2.3 GPA, so I kept pointing out the radical improvement in my grades during the last two years of undergrad.

Dean's list!

Provost honor roll!

Come on!

The second time I applied, I included a ridiculous number of letters of recommendation from transplant surgeons, faculty members, and colleagues. The admission officers decided that they would give me a chance and accepted me into the University of Miami's MBA program.

But that was it. I didn't get the tuition scholarship award for the MBA's $100,000-plus price tag, so I couldn't attend the program. Without the full tuition amount paid for with a scholarship, there would be no MBA for me.

The third time I applied, the admissions officers realized I wasn't going away.

They called me with a classic good news/bad news scenario. Good news: once again, I got into the MBA program. Bad news: they would only offer me a scholarship to cover 50 percent of the entire tuition package.

This time, as heartbreaking as it was, I did the rejecting.

It wasn't a matter of principle or pride. It was that every single dollar I made was going toward living expenses and repaying my parents and brother. I couldn't live with myself otherwise.

I said, "I just can't do it. I will keep trying until you guys give me the full scholarship, because I've been working for the University of Miami and teaching management courses to other employees. Eventually, I will earn the full hundred percent scholarship award."

I'll never know if they got sick of the prospect of processing my applications for the fourth time in four years or if what I said won them over.

What I do know is that a few hours later, the admissions officer called me back to say, "OK, Joe, you got it. One hundred percent of tuition paid for by the scholarship award. Welcome aboard!"

Every weekend for almost two years, I attended MBA classes while working full time during the week as the director of clinical operations at the University of Miami's OPO. I later learned that the year after I graduated from this program, the tuition remission award was no longer offered by the university due to the financial hardships of the great recession in 2008. Talk about luck!

If you can believe it, as of 2020, the architect and director of this prestigious program, Dr. Steve Ullmann, has invited me back to lecture to his class about organ donation and transplantation five years in a row, which is an incredible honor. To think that I almost didn't get in and now I am a guest lecturer at my dream school and the program I graduated from as a way to pay it forward while maintaining contact with influential leaders like Dr. Ullmann.

THE DAVITA STORY

Shortly before I graduated with my MBA, a company called DaVita began to recruit me for a senior leadership role. That position offered a higher title and salary than my current title and salary at the University of Miami's OPO.

As part of DaVita's recruitment process, candidates read case studies from the *Harvard Business Review* and Stanford's Graduate School of Business about the company's turnaround. (I recommend every business executive and leader read these.)

DaVita's against-all-odds turnaround is famous. The company underwent a remarkable transformation from a failing concern with poor management and grim company culture to consistent record-setting success and recognition as one of the country's most highly ranked company cultures. CEO Kent Thiry joined the company in 1999, facilitated its remarkable turnaround, and retired as its CEO in 2019. DaVita is studied and written about in MBA programs across the United States to this day.

DaVita offers kidney dialysis services at more than twenty-five hundred dialysis centers in the United States and hundreds of dialysis centers worldwide. The company's acquisition of Gambro, one of its largest competitors, essentially doubled the number of DaVita's employees from thirteen thousand to twenty-five thousand.

When Thiry was asked by his board of directors if he was excited about acquiring Gambro, he said, "Not at all." The Harvard Business School study notes, "He confessed that in spite of the strategic and financial benefits of the merger, he was afraid it might destroy the unique DaVita culture his team had created."[3]

Reading about Kent's focus on company culture made a lasting impact on me and informed the type of leader I am today. I'll discuss company culture in far more detail in chapter 6 ("Building a Successful Internal Culture: Two Steps Forward, One Step Back") and chapter 7 ("Eyes Wide Shut").

During DaVita's recruitment and interview process, the recruiter asked me if I would get the same satisfaction fulfilling DaVita's mission as I did from the mission of an OPO. I replied with the "right" answer, saying I would enjoy being part of DaVita's everyday mission, which was saving lives through dialysis as an overall part of making a positive difference in the world.

However, later that day, I reflected more thoughtfully on his question. I realized my passion for the OPO mission was all-encompassing and that I wanted to stay in the OPO space.

I DIDN'T KNOW IT AT THE TIME, BUT THIS WAS A VALUABLE LESSON IN CHOOSING YOUR ULTIMATE PASSION ABOVE ALL ELSE.

I turned the job opportunity at DaVita down. That was by no means an easy decision—it offered a grander title, a larger role, and a larger salary than my current situation at the University of Miami's OPO.

I didn't know it at the time, but this was a valuable lesson in choosing your ultimate passion above all else. I was grateful that the question posed to me by the recruiter helped me come to that conclusion.

---

3   William W. George and Natalie Kindred, "Kent Thiry: 'Mayor' of DaVita," *Harvard Business Review* (May 25, 2010, revised May 2, 2011).

THE WAITING GAME

I graduated with an MBA in 2009 with a 3.7 GPA. Perseverance had paid off.

As I was acutely aware, there are only fifty-eight OPO executive director/president/CEO positions in the United States. (The titles for the top leadership positions at OPOs vary. For context, I'm the president and CEO of the Nevada Donor Network OPO; the title of my boss at the University of Miami's OPO was executive director.)

In one sense, I was fortunate to work at the University of Miami's OPO, as it is one of only six in the country affiliated with a larger institution. I benefited immensely from opportunities and interaction with attendant resources that are part of a larger institution and the chance to learn from a wide variety of individuals across a multitude of professions.

But as an MBA graduate, I could do the math: fifty-eight OPOs meant only fifty-eight potential top-spot opportunities.

At a well-run OPO—or any well-run organization, regardless of industry—there's usually an established succession plan for when the head of the organization steps down. I could continue to aim to become the University of Miami's OPO's executive director, its highest leadership position. However, the executive director of an affiliated OPO doesn't have the same freedom and opportunities as the CEO of a stand-alone, nonaffiliated OPO.

The top person at an affiliated OPO has five or more bosses above them. They are subject to the budget constraints of that institution, such as hiring freezes and myriad other issues that come with being part of a large and multifaceted organization. It is virtually impossible to act entrepreneurially in that environment.

Also, my boss at the University of Miami OPO was not planning to retire anytime soon. Still, I was willing to wait for the opportunity to pursue a leadership position in the OPO space, and ideally at the specific OPO where I was currently working, its affiliation with the University notwithstanding. (After all, that affiliation had been a tremendously positive force in my life for more than a decade.)

OPO FYI

OPOs in the United States are all 501(c)3 not-for-profit organizations, irrespective of affiliation with a larger institution, and all OPOs operate under the federal government's oversight—specifically, the Organ Procurement and Transplantation Network (OPTN), a national transplant network established by federal law (the National Organ Transplant Act of 1984). As described in the introduction, the OPTN is managed by the United Network for Organ Sharing (UNOS), a private nonprofit organization that manages the nation's organ transplant system under contract with the federal government.

Every transplant hospital, organ procurement organization, and transplant histocompatibility laboratory in the United States is an OPTN member. Membership means that an institution meets the OPTN requirements to be a member.

Because of the federally mandated aspect of OPOs, when anything significant occurs, such as ongoing poor performance, it is publicly recorded. I'd already sat on several OPTN/UNOS committees, so I was pretty aware of anything significant that happened in the OPO space.

At the OPTN/UNOS board meeting in June 2011, for the first time in history, an OPO—the Nevada Donor Network—was declared a "Member Not in Good Standing."[4]

---

4   "Nevada Donor Network declared a member not in good standing," US Department of Health and Human Services—Organ Procurement and Transplantation Network, press release, July 9, 2011, https://optn. transplant.hrsa.gov/news/nevada-donor-network-declared-a-member-not-in-good-standing/.

SUMMARY OF EVENTS (FROM THE PRESS RELEASE ISSUED BY THE OPTN)

UNOS staff conducted four OPTN compliance surveys at the Nevada Donor Network between November 2008 and December 2010. These included two on-site surveys by UNOS staff, a desk survey by UNOS staff, and a peer visit conducted by two organ donation professionals assisted by UNOS staff. In response to these issues, the MPSC undertook a systematic due process review, which included an interview with representatives of the Nevada Donor Network on March 11, 2011. The MPSC recommended the Nevada Donor Network to be designated an OPTN Member Not in Good Standing. As part of its regularly scheduled June 2011 meeting, the OPTN/UNOS board of directors approved the MPSC's recommendation. The Organ Procurement and Transplantation Network (OPTN) is operated under contract with the US Department of Health and Human Services, Health Resources and Services Administration, Division of Transplantation by the United Network for Organ Sharing (UNOS). The OPTN brings together medical professionals, transplant recipients, and donor families to develop organ transplantation policy.

I knew about the issues at the NDN, thanks to the small and public nature of the OPO community.

I knew something else: that the NDN was looking for a new president and CEO of the organization. I decided to apply.

CHAPTER 4

ON THIN ICE

On the one hand, applying for the president and CEO role of the NDN was a no-brainer, for the reasons I outlined in the previous chapter. An opportunity to lead an OPO is rare.

And I was impatient to apply my MBA-enhanced career skills to new and more significant challenges than the ones I was encountering at the University of Miami's OPO.

On the other hand, the NDN was a hot mess.

AOPO

The Association of Organ Procurement Organizations (AOPO) is a voluntary accreditation program with standards that encompass all aspects of organ procurement organization (OPO) operations and practice. It consists of a peer review process that assesses compliance with the AOPO standards and helps OPOs meet federal regulations as set forth by the OPTN/UNOS.

CMS

The Center for Medicare and Medicaid Services (CMS) provides guidance for affiliated Medicare and Medicaid services. CMS also certifies an OPO for a specific service area.

The NDN had a new and unique "Member Not in Good Standing" designation, lost its AOPO accreditation, and was non-compliant with CMS standards.

Adding to general confusion and dysfunction, the NDN's administration at the time insisted that the loss of AOPO accreditation and lack of compliance with the CMS did not risk the NDN's operations.

One hundred percent incorrect.

Voluntary or not, the loss of an AOPO accreditation was a big red flag to the OPTN/UNOS and the industry. So was NDN's noncompliance with CMS guidelines. The "Member Not in Good Standing" designation by the OPTN/UNOS was a direct result of those flags.

It's fair to ask where the NDN's board of directors was while all this was going on. As a nonprofit, the NDN's board of directors is a voluntary fy (unlike for-profit institutions, in which the board members get paid to sit and participate on a board). These were mostly a great group of well-meaning individuals who wanted to be involved with a nonprofit and cared deeply about the community the NDN benefited. They trusted the leadership to tell them the truth, given that most of them didn't have in-depth experience with the intricacies and rigid guidelines to which OPOs must adhere.

The egregious abuse of their trust by certain individuals was practically criminal.

What the board of directors, and eventually I, discovered was that previous leadership was selectively sharing information to avoid being held accountable. They were painting a rosy picture rather than an accurate blood-red picture, reflecting a level of hemorrhaging that is often a harbinger of imminent death.

When the board of directors finally realized that what they were hearing from leadership was irreconcilable with common sense, they did all the right things. They exited the long-term CEO, put an interim consultant CEO in place, and began a search for a permanent president and CEO.

A HOT MESS

Long before I heard of the NDN opportunity, I remember sitting in meetings at the University of Miami's OPO discussing the infamous goings-on at the NDN. We were continually shocked by the NDN's embarrassingly poor performance. There was community-wide speculation that the NDN might be the first OPO in history to get shut down.

By 2011 the NDN had alienated everyone due to its grievous inability to fulfill its most basic functions. Everyone was used to its extreme level of incompetence. The entire OPO community, including the OPTN/UNOS, AOPO, and CMS, knew not to believe any commitment or metric value put forth by the administration of NDN in place at the time.

It was a terrible situation. There was nothing timely or efficient about the obtention of healthy donor organs and tissues, which meant that in most cases, they weren't obtained at all. Internally, people felt utterly demoralized and paranoid. They had no resources or incentives designed to support the organization's mission; doing so would have necessitated pointing out myriad issues and barriers to success—inviting swift retribution.

As you just learned, the NDN's board of directors experienced a series of painful shocks upon discovering the large disconnect between reality and what they were being told. Additional discoveries uncovered a horrific management style and a company culture rife with toxicity and fear.

CULTURE, CULTURE, CULTURE

We all know the three most important considerations in real estate.

Location, location, location.

With companies, the answer is similar.

It's culture, culture, culture.

A nonempathetic culture is one of many reasons the previous incarnation of the Nevada Donor Network didn't succeed. The leadership team was old school, managing by punitive whim. People would be hired, fired, transferred, promoted, or shut out, depending on the administration's mood of the moment.

The administration made all the decisions and conveyed them as orders to employees, an opaque process that gave people little insight into how or why those decisions were made. People felt undervalued and unsupported by the leadership team. It got to the point where employees would come in and just hang out in an upstairs lounge area for hours to run out the clock on their day. They felt bad about doing that, but in their minds, it was better than doing work that wasn't understood, appreciated, or supported. There was a lot of siloed behavior, where some departments wouldn't know what the others were doing.

Speaking up about the impact mismanagement had on the organization, its community partners, and heroic donors and transplant recipients invited punishment.

People in the organization eventually got the message: the only way forward was to keep their mouths shut, or only to open them to agree with those in charge, no matter how ill advised a direction or initiative they proposed. Within the NDN, employees who couldn't stomach that ethos worked while feeling miserable until they got fired or left as a matter of principle.

By the time I got to the NDN, there was still a core of people dedicated to its mission but stymied on how they could make a difference. The toxic environment prevented anyone from achieving much.

In late 2011 the longtime CEO was ushered out by the board, the interim CEO from the donation and transplantation industry and formerly with HHS stepped in as a consultant (flying in from another state where she lived), and the NDN's board of directors began its search for a permanent president and CEO. This is when discussions with me for the position began, punctuated by long silences.

Despite the NDN's deplorable condition, I was still determined to pursue the role as its new president and CEO. It wasn't an obvious decision. I was essentially the Miami OPO's clinical COO. I wouldn't have considered leaving the organization for a lateral move. It isn't uncommon that when you spend most of your career at one organization, especially a large and bureaucratic one, no matter how successful you are, you experience a sense of limited advancement potential. In my case, I knew that wasn't an accurate reflection of my achievements to date—I had fully earned the respect and responsibility that came with my role. At the same time, I couldn't help but wonder if the people who would eventually review my application for the executive director position at the University of Miami's OPO would be able to center their perception of where I was, rather than where I'd started as a young technician.

Finally, I was impatient. I wanted to lead an entire organization. The story of Ken Thiry's spectacular turnaround of company culture—and company results—at DaVita inspired me. I wanted to do something similar. Here was such an opportunity.

The NDN was a flailing organization. Its culture was toxic, and its operations were so poor that it was under a shutdown threat specifically created to address its issues.

The role of president and CEO of the NDN was an opportunity—and crystallization of the previously mentioned Winston Churchill quote, "Never let a good crisis go to waste."

I wasn't going to.

In late 2011 I sent an application letter applying for the president and CEO role at the NDN. Usually when you apply for that type of role, you at least get an acknowledgment of your application. I got crickets.

A week later, I sent a follow-up note, this time with detail that I thought would prove to be useful to the board of directors. I included an analysis of how the NDN was perceived industry-wide as compared to other OPOs.

The NDN's board was, as I said, staffed with well-meaning individuals. But they lacked awareness, insight, and institutional expertise specific to the OPO space. The data I shared illustrated how the NDN (and Miami's OPO) ranked against a national dashboard—one that showed all the key consistent metrics that each OPO measures itself (or should measure itself) against to determine how well it is performing in its mission. On this national dashboard I shared, NDN ranked fifty-seventh out of fifty-eight OPOs in the country in terms of performance. Almost dead last. So they had that going for them.

By this point, the board of directors wasn't surprised by the NDN's poor showing, and the point of the exercise was not to belabor that issue. They were grateful for the context, transparency, and education about how the OPO industry monitored and managed itself. This was information they should have had all along.

Sharing a national dashboard provided valuable context about the industry that helped the board of directors best understand the metrics and indicators used to evaluate an OPO. It got the ball rolling in terms of more active and serious conversations about the strategy and tactics I would utilize—specifically, being open and transparent about how the data defining the NDN ranked against national metrics. My enthusiasm for turning the situation around, based on my COO-level responsibilities at the University of Miami's OPO—showed how I'd utilize data to keep the NDN moving in the right direction and communicate with the board of directors to keep them informed.

CAPTAIN JOE

I met with the board of directors multiple times. At one meeting, several board members were very interested in the fact that I had a United States Coast Guard (USCG) Master Captain's license. They wanted to know more about what inspired me to pursue a USCG Master Captain's license, which is a pretty high-level and intense process that most recreational boaters don't usually pursue. It is meant for hired captains of very large vessels.

That I wanted to achieve the highest level of expertise in an area I was passionate about made an impression on them. I think it drove home that I'd always aim for the highest possible level of expertise that would allow me to execute my responsibilities to their ultimate potential.

We talked about the qualities a successful captain must possess that were also applicable to the role of president and CEO of an organization.

I said this: "When you're on a boat, a lot of bad things can happen. There are some dangerous parts of navigating a boat where you're at the mercy of the ocean, and as captain you have to adapt, rapidly and expertly, to adjust to changing conditions and change your course to ensure the safety of the passengers and crew along with a successful outcome of the voyage." I shared a gripping story about what it was like to captain a boat in the Gulf Stream before sophisticated GPS tools were part of everyday boating equipment. The Gulf Stream between Florida and the Bahamas covers a relatively short path (fifty miles).

Those fifty miles make up one of the most treacherous and complex water routes in the world, part of the famous Bermuda Triangle. Currents consistently push or pull (or both at the same time!) your boat from the course it needs to take. Severe thunderstorms pop up without notice, given the warm waters and dramatic temperature changes. There are no visual landmarks behind you (Miami) or in front of you (the Bahamas). You must keep moving and constantly keep track of your position—not only where you're going but also where you've been. The weather and current will constantly try to knock you off course, so you must constantly keep your eye on the compass to track your true north and bearing to your destination.

I told the board of directors all about the other dangers boating captains around Miami and the Bahamas dealt with: We had to be worried about fires or rough waves that would cause the boat to take on water and sink. There were storms for which you could not prepare for but had to navigate through. There were even pirates! Seriously! It was a really dangerous time to captain a boat in that area. Pirates would hijack a boat, strip it of expensive equipment, and sometimes kill everyone on board before taking the boat out of the region to the remote Bahamas or even Cuba. That's why many boaters elected to travel in groups.

Being aware of risks, adjusting to them, and being as proactive as possible to mitigate issues are key skills, whether you're at the helm of a boat or an organization. The most important thing, I stressed, is that the person in charge must always stay true to their compass and vision while taking care of the passengers and crew.

On my way back to the room to continue our conversation, I heard one board member say, "Captain Joe is going to figure out how to do this. He's our guy." I know—the irony. A USCG Master Captain in the middle of the Nevada desert.

MAN PLANS, GOD LAUGHS

The entire process from my initial application to my acceptance of the position took six months. In March 2012, I signed an employment contract with the NDN, accepting my new position as the president and CEO of the Nevada Donor Network.

> THE MOST IMPORTANT THING, I STRESSED, IS THAT THE PERSON IN CHARGE MUST ALWAYS STAY TRUE TO THEIR COMPASS AND VISION WHILE TAKING CARE OF THE PASSENGERS AND CREW.

I was excited to get started at the NDN, but I also wanted to give a full month's worth of attention to ensuring a smooth transition for my team and department at the University of Miami's OPO. I announced my resignation on March 5 and planned to start at the NDN on April 16. Everything was in place, and I had enough time to prepare for my new role at the NDN and transition my responsibilities at the Miami OPO.

Then I got a phone call from the chair of the NDN's board of directors, a lovely woman named Kathy Crabtree in healthcare management who had been forthright and supportive throughout the entire interview process. Thanks to her and the board in place at the time, I was going to get my shot at running an OPO.

She had lots of news, and none of it was good.

The interim consultant CEO felt that the vice president of clinical affairs, whom she found obdurate, should be fired before my arrival so I could hit the ground running without significant opposition.

The board of directors declined to let the interim CEO fire the vice president of clinical affairs. This infuriated the interim CEO, who quit on the spot during a board meeting. The vice president of clinical affairs also resigned the next day, unbeknownst to the newly departed interim CEO.

All of this occurred less than three weeks before I was due to take over the reins at the NDN.

The board was required to hurriedly put a second interim CEO in place until my imminent arrival. They selected someone who was a member of the board with private-industry executive experience, who graciously filled in for a few weeks before I arrived. He was a passionate member of the board and a savvy entrepreneur with a great business acumen. He is also a heart transplant recipient of more than thirty years. His connection to and passionate advocacy for the mission served as one of the catalysts for change in the leadership of the NDN, which led to my being hired as its fearless leader.

Less than a month before I was to join the NDN, the organization was leaderless and rudderless, since the newly departed vice president of clinical affairs was the most OPO-experienced executive and responsible for a significant segment of the OPO operations at the NDN.

But that wasn't all. There was more.

THE STRAW THAT (ALMOST) BROKE THE CAMEL'S BACK

When there are critical leadership changes at an OPO, the organization must notify the OPTN/UNOS within a certain period. The board of directors duly notified UNOS of the interim CEO's and vice president of clinical affairs' resignations.

All this upheaval resulted in a letter from UNOS that said, in part, "Due to the instability of the organization and the leadership dynamics, the Membership and Professional Standard Committee is considering removing Nevada Donor Network as a member of UNOS."

The letter demanded a response by April 16, 2012, my original start date.

What the MPSC said, but in more political terms, was this: "You guys are done. There's no way you can turn this around. It doesn't matter if Joe's coming on board or not. That's why we're threatening to remove your membership, because you've claimed to have been on a corrective action plan for a year. You've now gone through an original CEO, an interim CEO, and the vice president of clinical affairs, and now you have a new interim CEO for a few weeks who has no OPO experience. We're seriously considering removing you as a member."

That was the most significant threat the NDN had received to date. It was 100 percent warranted.

But what was really on my mind was this: the Nevada Donor Network, the organization I had just joined as president and CEO, had just been told it was about to be shut down permanently. A thoughtful, detailed, and genuine response had to be created and sent to the OPTN/MPSC by April 16.

The board chair shared that in light of these new developments, the board of directors worried I would change my mind about joining the NDN as its president and CEO.

Her call did make me think, but not for long.

The board chair and I had an open and transparent conversation, given that the situation had worsened significantly since I had accepted the position of president and CEO. We hammered out a revised agreement with added severance and safeguards if I could not turn things around, given the threat level and time limitations. I stayed firm on my decision to join the NDN as president and CEO, despite the very real possibility that the entity would be shut down by the federal government.

The one point I insisted upon was hiring a Washington, DC–based legal firm, one familiar with OPO regulations and machinations. They were experienced and savvy. Nothing I had seen or heard to date about the NDN's legal advisors signaled that they were experts in OPO regulatory policy. I wasn't going to start our most important communication and subsequent interactions—ones that would determine if the NDN had a future—without industry-experienced counsel I could trust. I wanted our legal support aligned with my intention, to be honest about mistakes made to date and transparent about the short- and long-term plans to improve the situation. The lead attorney I hired with the NDN board's support, named Stuart Langbein, was an attorney very familiar with our industry and came highly recommended by my former executive boss, Leslie.

This was the organizational leadership challenge I had been waiting for.

When Kent Thiry took on the role of CEO at DaVita, he knew things were bad at the company. When he got into the position, he found out things were far worse than he had realized. It appeared that a similar situation was happening here.

I felt as ready as I would ever be to take the reins. I wanted to serve as the leader this organization desperately needed.

I took a deep breath, changed my ticket, and flew to Las Vegas to start my new job as president and CEO of the worst-performing OPO in the world.

CHAPTER 5

TRIAGE

The enormous scale of the NDN's systemic dysfunction drove the OPTN officials and the MPSC to consider doing something they had never done before. In the entire history of the OPO industry, an OPO never had been threatened with removal as a member. The MPSC's letter reiterated why the NDN would potentially be the first.

Our response to this letter took precedence over everything else and required me to start my tenure as the president and CEO of the NDN at its moment of supreme crisis.

LIMITED OPTIONS

The MPSC gave the NDN a blunt choice: engage in good faith with the MPSC, or accept its recommendation to shut down the organization and turn our responsibilities over to another OPO.

So much weighed on our initial response to the MPSC letter, which included eleven sets of pointed questions that required detailed response. A few of the questions are shared below. They highlight how the previous approach of not engaging with MPSC fully, and not sharing timely or comprehensive updates regarding corrective actions, created a complete lack of faith in the NDN's ability to course-correct its downward trajectory.

Our response—the first communication I would make as the president and CEO of the NDN—was an opportunity to demonstrate how the new leadership team was going to communicate and operate according to regulatory industry guidelines.

> *Question: How is the NDN ensuring effective day-to-day operations at the present time, given the current vacancy in leadership? Specifically, who is providing clinical oversight of operations? How is the NDN ensuring that staff and frontline supervisors or managers have access to senior clinical leadership on a twenty-four seven basis? Who is serving managerial or leader-level "on call" functions? Please describe the leader-on-call rotation.*

This was the very first set of questions on the list. The NDN had not given MPSC—or external stakeholders within the OPO industry at large—any evidence whatsoever of its leadership team's breadth and functionality. That the OPTN/MPSC needed to ask for this level of detail and assurance was embarrassing. (Note: The MPSC is the body that acts on behalf of and as part of the OPTN board, which is the peer review compliance authority for OPOs. The MPSC makes recommendations that are sent to the OPTN board of directors for vote/approval.) These questions highlighted the NDN's failure to provide comprehensive and effective support for its most critical functions and create practical solutions to address that lack.

> *What is the NDN's plan to ensure proper training or support of their new key leaders, particularly training and support in the NDN's clinical and quality/safety processes, the current*

corrective action plan in place for the OPTN, and OPTN compliance expectations? How will the NDN assure that the new CEO and VP of clinical services, as well as other new leaders, are given proper orientation, training, and support? Our concern is that effective training is unlikely to occur from within the organization, so how will the NDN boards (directors and medical) ensure the competency of key leaders?

This second set of questions shows extraordinary and justified skepticism of the capabilities and competencies of employees who had joined the NDN in the previous eighteen months. Many hires were managers with little to no experience in the OPO space. Experienced leaders in the OPO space were well aware of the NDN's pervasive issues and didn't want to go anywhere near the organization.

The new hires failed at designing, implementing, and maintaining effective corrective action plans. That was understandable, as they had no in-depth knowledge of the OPO space. Their failures—and the ongoing tolerance of failures by the executive leadership team—were further indications of the organization's many issues.

Please provide data as to how many local organ donor referrals and recoveries have been handled and their results, including numbers of organs recovered and transplanted since inception of your corrective action plan (CAP) last fall. How many of those were DCD? The OPTN needs to review your performance measures indicating status of your local donor operations.

This telling question references a CAP initiative that began in the fall of 2011, designed to ensure more effective management of organ referrals and recoveries. It shows that the OPTN had not been provided with updates and data that could testify to the success, or lack thereof, of that particular CAP since its inception six months earlier.

The OPTN had repeatedly asked the NDN to provide comprehensive quarterly updates about all significant CAPs. NDN's lack of willingness and ability to do so was another red flag in a sea of them. It was an additional example of a leadership team unwilling to engage with regulators or themselves in a process designed to improve operations.

> *The CAP summary for February states that during review of labeling accuracy, errors were not being reported, and data may be inaccurate. Is there any additional information available on how many errors may have been missed?*

NDN's poor monitoring of CAPs and communication of the same with the OPTN was in part due to a bizarre conspiracy theory: that a neighboring OPO was somehow orchestrating the NDN's downfall to gain control over Nevada's donor supply. Unfortunately, one of the people who believed in this theory was one of NDN's long-term external legal advisors.

This person had no OPO industry experience and had no idea how absurd this conspiracy idea was. The NDN failures were 100 percent a product of internal mismanagement. Nonetheless, counsel used the theory as a rationale for recommending a nonengagement and guarded strategy with the OPTN peer reviewers.

The misguided strategy of providing the OPTN/MPSC with minimal and incomplete information sabotaged the NDN's ability to work with the regulatory body responsible for deciding if it would be allowed to survive or shut down.

TRANSPARENCY AND IMMEDIACY

It would have been entirely understandable to ask the MPSC for a continuance, given I had just joined the NDN and wanted time to find my sea legs.

However, asking for more time didn't seem to be the right play.

The NDN had dug itself deeply into a hole with a playbook based on denials, deflections, and a persistent disinclination to engage with the OPTN/MPSC. Externally, the NDN's reputation was shattered. Internally, the culture was completely fragmented.

I knew my first step as the president and CEO of the organization would have to be significant and indicative of how the NDN was going to change, in part by addressing issues immediately, head on, and with full transparency.

Our communication style and rehabilitation efforts needed to demonstrate how the NDN would do things differently moving forward. We had to practice open and frequent communication with the OPTN/MPSC and with ourselves, in a good-faith effort to fix the myriad issues at the organization. Every single internal and external communication and action had to show that we were fully engaged in enabling the NDN to fulfill its mission as successfully as possible.

We responded to the MPSC on time with comprehensive and detailed responses to all of their questions. Our cover letter, from me, was transparent about the situation, my extensive OPO experience, and my familiarity with regulations, and it cited a team effort dedicated to achieving a new standard of compliance and successful operations at the NDN.

We designed the letter to draw attention to one thing: *everything* about how the NDN communicated and functioned would be different and better.

As you may know, my first date of employment as president/ CEO at NDN was April 11, 2012. This has only afforded five calendar days to evaluate current operations and the status of the NDN corrective action plan (CAP) since my arrival. As a result, I have considered the prospect of a request to you and the MPSC for an extension to provide this response attached hereto; however, it is obvious that the NDN has fallen short of previous MPSC expectations and CAP deadlines in the recent past. In good faith, I have decided not to request an extension so as not to convey a lack of accountability and responsiveness on the part of NDN to the MPSC and the OPTN board of directors. I have diligently worked with current key leaders in the last five days to prepare the response to this inquiry to the best of my knowledge at this point in my role at the NDN. Although my time as part of the NDN team has been brief, it is apparent based on the documents I have reviewed and my extensive experience in OPO operations, regulatory compliance, and quality management that there is much work to be done, expeditiously. I can assure you that the process of taking accountability and decisive action to correct the current state of affairs is rigorously underway, and I am committed to applying my experience and knowledge to improve NDN on behalf of the donors, their families, and the recipients we serve as stewards of this critical mission. The NDN Governing Board, Medical Advisory Board, and the staff at NDN have pledged full support in these efforts, and we all look forward to living up to the expectations of the MPSC, the OPTN board of directors, and the stakeholders we serve going forward.

The OPTN/MPSC informed the NDN that our fate would be determined at an MPSC meeting in July. We would have a chance to make a short fifteen-minute presentation about the changes in the organization, participate in a merciless Q&A, and then learn whether we would be granted a stay of execution or shut down.

In the three months before the MPSC meeting, we had to rapidly formulate, implement, and communicate radically different CAPs to effect visible and sustainable changes that would impel the answer we wanted.

You've heard that sunlight is the best disinfectant? NDN's diseased culture was about to be disinfected by the uncomfortable inclusion of our critics, big time. It would not be pretty or quick, but it was the only way forward.

We were going to illuminate and own every single issue and mistake, offer root-cause analysis that explained why

> WE WOULD FOCUS ON DOING THAT ONE THING—WHICH IS TO SAY, *EVERYTHING*—DIFFERENTLY AND BETTER.

our system allowed for issues, share CAPs designed to prevent similar problems, and track metrics to show whether a CAP was a success or required additional refinement. By doing this we demonstrated accountability for our past and that we were receptive to inclusion of our most vocal critics in the spirit of making things better for the community we served. Furthermore, we were going to communicate all of this information consistently to all key stakeholders, ensuring everyone was current with what was happening at the NDN.

We would focus on doing that one thing—which is to say, *everything*—differently and better. Because July 25, 2012, was our very last chance to prove to the OPTN/MPSC that we could turn the NDN around.

YOU CAN'T MAKE THIS STUFF UP

The initial letter from the MPSC wasn't the only surprise at the start of my tenure at NDN. But it was undoubtedly the biggest, putting us on notice that we were in a fight for survival.

During my first few months at the NDN, while preparing for the meeting that would determine the organization's fate, I was confronted with additional surprises.

Out of Office and PTO

On my first day in the office, the director of human resources was on vacation. She was on vacation for two weeks: the week I arrived and the week after I joined. I had started five days early, but still …

When a new CEO comes in to take charge of an organization undergoing tremendous upheaval, the head of HR should be present. I realized that her actions were a product of the environment that had developed at the NDN and decided not to make an issue of it and give her the benefit of the doubt. Then, while I was going over administrative items, I noticed she hadn't registered her vacation days as paid time off (PTO).

When asked why, she told me about NDN's vacation/PTO policy. If an employee worked for at least fifteen minutes a day—and checking emails remotely counted!—then the employee could count that day as a full day's work and didn't have to submit it as a vacation day or PTO. I was shocked.

That policy is no longer in place.

Overtime

Clinical staff at the NDN (and most OPOs) are paid hourly. When they work overtime, they get paid more. As a result, the NDN had several clinical staffers whose annual salaries were higher than some directors. (Some of those extra hours were padded; most were legitimate. We quickly weeded out those who abused the overtime policy.) Prior to my arrival, the directors had approached NDN administration and demanded that they also be paid hourly. That was so they could register overtime and "catch up" or make more than clinical staffers.

That behavior is antithetical to what one expects to see in a sophisticated organization with a functional CEO and thoughtful head of HR. The lack of judgment was astounding. No one in a management position at an organization should be paid hourly, let alone for such a petty reason.

I disbanded that policy within a short time of my arrival. I told all directors and managers that they were immediately considered exempt (that is, employees with a salary, not eligible for overtime).

Batteries

The inventory process for the organization was abysmal. One of the functions the interim CEO had taken over was to go through every invoice and approve it. Normally, someone in office management or finance handles this kind of work, not the CEO. However, that was the process in place when I arrived. I prioritized the issues I had to fix, and this was not high on my list.

I'd spend an hour each week looking at shipping logs and order invoices. I noticed the NDN was ordering an absurd number of batteries—just regular AA, AAA, C, D, and DD batteries—hundreds of dollars' worth every month. The NDN is a regular office, and no office needs the number of batteries we were ordering. It didn't make any sense.

Our accounting manager didn't know what all the batteries were for; she guessed they were to power the wireless mice or maybe the remote controls of various devices in the office. She wasn't trying to deceive me; she just didn't know. Her job wasn't forensic accounting; it was to pay the invoices once the CEO OK'd them.

It turned out the interim CEO hadn't taken the time to review the invoices individually (totally understandable—it was a time-wasting and exhausting exercise); instead, she just rubber-stamped them as approved.

As a result, some employees realized they could treat the NDN ordering system like their own personal Home Depot. And they did, with the help of a complicit employee who was in charge of office inventory.

I couldn't believe I had to do this. I sent out a communication to all departments saying, "OK, from now on, before anybody orders batteries, I need to know about it because I need to figure out what we're ordering all of these batteries for."

The next week the number of batteries ordered by the NDN went to zero, and no wireless mice were harmed in the changing of the policy.

Gift Cards

While I was dealing with the great battery mystery, another inventory abuse was taking place.

The NDN would purchase coffee shop gift cards to hand out to hospital team members who would help us. The person in charge of inventory would routinely keep ten out of one hundred cards for himself. He told another employee what he was doing, suggesting they do the same, saying management would never know.

The other employee told a member of the management team what was going on. We quickly fired the head inventory personnel.

All of these issues—and more—took place during my initial few months at the NDN. I was so consumed with nervous energy that I started micromanaging as much as I could. I couldn't take the chance the NDN would mess up in such a way that would shut down all of our efforts prior to our life-or-death meeting with the MPSC.

SURVEYING THE LANDSCAPE

Soon after I took the reins at the NDN, I sent a short six-question survey to all upper-management team members.

SURVEY QUESTIONS

Aside from the current UNOS/CMS issues, what are the biggest challenges the organization is facing or will face in the near future?

Why do you think the organization is facing these challenges?

What are the most unexploited opportunities for growth?

What do you feel would need to happen for the organization to exploit these opportunities?

If you were me, what would you focus your attention on?

Open question: Please list any other accolades, positives, issues, or concerns that you think I should know about in any aspect of NDN, including staff, vendors, colleagues, relationships, etc.

The answers consistently cited the NDN's siloed and splintered culture as the organization's biggest challenge. There was no unity or support from leadership team members or across different departments. The organization's toxic culture, built on blame, obfuscation, refusal to take accountability, plus lack of support for and follow-through on strong corrective actions, severely hampered its ability to function effectively.

On the plus side, people recognized ample opportunities for the NDN to repair and improve its function.

There was a common denominator to the issues described: company culture. The thoughtful answers identified the five key areas on which the success or failure of the NDN depended:

- **Donation process not being maximized.** We were not handling this critical component (indeed, the OPO's raison d'être) effectively. Our interactions with hospital staff and families were sloppy and inconsistent. We were missing multiple opportunities to connect with potential heroic donors and their families in a timely manner (which would maximize our reach to all possible healthy organs and tissues).

- **Underreporting "imminent and eligible" referrals.** Because of our poor relationships with local hospitals, and our slow and sloppy follow-up procedures, we often underreported the number of "imminent and eligible" donor referrals that required timely attention to ensure they were cared for and diligently managed, and that the vital organs were recovered, packaged properly, and delivered promptly.

- **Inadequate hospital development DSA-wide plan and strategy.** DSA stands for Donation Service Area, a federally designated area where a CMS-certified OPO coordinates activities. The NDN had lost its CMS compliance and had no meaningful structure to guide its interactions with hospitals in our DSA. Our poor interactions with hospitals in our DSA directly resulted in our underreporting imminent and eligible donor referrals, and our overall inability to maximize the donation process.

The last two points need no explanation.

- **Operational performance substandard.**

- **Governance and accountability deficient.**

TRANSPARENCY AND VULNERABILITY

Our detailed document outlined every single existing issue, with most issues identified as a "*New* Area for Continuous Improvement."

Those words were chosen advisedly.

The use of the word *new* called attention to problems previously unexamined within the organization and unreported to the OPTN.

This document was radically different from anything anyone at the NDN had worked on before. It was unflinching in its overview of issues, planned resolutions, and rigid adherence to metrics we would use to measure success.

We outlined each issue; our goal of creating an ongoing effective function; a CAP; a brief explanation of how the situation came to be; the date by which we expected our solution to be up and running; and the metrics and monitoring systems used to indicate success or need for additional adjustment. All of this would be communicated relentlessly, inside the NDN and, externally, to the OPTN.

I fully ascribe to Peter Drucker's philosophy: "What gets measured gets done. What gets measured publicly gets done faster."

We shared this extensive document, consisting of thirty-five meaty CAPs, with the OPTN one month prior to the MPSC meeting. It gave the MPSC ample time to review the steps we had taken and context to the claims we would make during our July presentation.

Example:

NEW AREA FOR CONTINUOUS IMPROVEMENT	The current staffing structure of organ recovery, hospital development, and family services staff is not consistent with other high-performing OPOs and may benefit from specialization of roles for critical processes.
OVERARCHING GOAL	**Restructure Organ Recovery, Hospital Development, and Family Services staff to allow for optimal training and support of critical donation processes with specialized staff.**
CORRECTIVE ACTION #1	Develop the Role of Surgical Recovery Coordinator as a specialist in the Operating Room environment who will facilitate surgical assistance, organ preservation, packaging, labeling, and transport of organs/tissues to support Procurement Transplant Coordinator (PTC) role.
EXPLANATION	The current NDN recovery process relies on the PTC role for optimal donor management and for all duties in the Operating Room environment related to the organ donation and recovery process. The primary weakness of this model is the overextension of the PTC role with expectations of expertise in ICU patient optimization for maximum donation yield and careful coordination of the surgical recovery process, which involves technical tasks. The SRC role will be composed of highly trained staff who would be solely responsible for the process of surgical organ recovery, packaging, and transport of the organs as needed. It is thought that this role will facilitate continued compliance and improvement in the packaging and labeling of organs in accordance with OPTN policy.
COMPLETION DATE	September 1, 2012
METRICS AND MONITORING	Employee scorecards, NDN internal audit process, and employee performance evaluations.

The contrast to NDN's previous documentation and CAPs was immediately apparent. Prior to my arrival, NDN's sparse communications placed the blame for the company's failings on external partners.

We did not. The information we collected and shared stressed internal accountability.

There were no Band-Aid corrections. This was the reverse of a Band-Aid fix: we were ripping all the Band-Aids off, exposing everything to everyone. Internally, we saw it all. Externally, we shared everything with the OPTN/MPSC.

In the spirit of transparency and vulnerability, we acknowledged a long history of broken promises to internal and external stakeholders. For us to be successful in the eyes of ourselves, our partners in the OPO community, and the OPTN/MPSC, we had to keep our promises and engage in constant communication that showed we were implementing rapid, decisive, and sustainable changes.

LIFE BY COMMITTEE

An MPSC meeting is intense. It's like a Senate hearing for the OPO industry: it takes place in a very large room with official representatives from a multitude of industry organizations and peer groups.

It can be intimidating and nerve-racking, especially if you're there to address a number of embarrassing issues.

On July 25, 2012, I flew to Chicago to present the NDN's argument for continued existence. I didn't go alone. The NDN's director of quality services, director of organ recovery, assistant director of organ recovery, director of family and hospital, director of finance/human resources, and two members of our board of directors came to the MPSC meeting with me. These senior leaders were responsible for our major departments and teams.

It was important for the NDN senior management team to attend and participate in the MPSC meeting. It's one thing for the CEO to say, "I know exactly what we need to do. We need to do this, this, and this," but it's another thing to have the entire team in the room.

Colleagues of mine who served on the OPTN committees gave

me a lot of advice about handling this critical meeting. One point they hammered home was that the committee hadn't seen or heard from NDN management. The only communications the MPSC received were from counsel and were deliberately oblique.

Having the team participate and speak to the changes we were making allowed the MPSC to see the leadership team's full-scale engagement. We had to show that the entire NDN management team understood and respected the process. Otherwise, our argument that the NDN had changed for the better wasn't going to fly.

The presentation to the MPSC, delivered by me, could only be fifteen minutes long. The real tough time would be during the extensive Q&A session. The management team and I spent a lot of time with our experienced counsel, participating in mock Q&As to prepare.

Prior to the meeting, we took every opportunity to share updates—good, bad, and always supported with comprehensive detail—with the OPTN/MPSC. We took every opportunity to demonstrate that the NDN practices had changed, that the organization was engaging in implementing successful and sustainable solutions. For example, one month before the MPSC meeting, UNOS staff conducted a surprise visit to the NDN on behalf of the OPTN/MPSC. The subsequent report cited several issues that we immediately addressed in a detailed response two weeks after the visit. Following our established format (created in accordance with the UNOS preferred template), we acknowledged each issue, explained our findings on how it occurred, and detailed the CAPs we put in place to address it.

THE PRESENTATION

The fifteen-minute presentation, informed by the survey from my first weeks at the NDN, covered our five key pillars from the vantage point of the past, present, and future.

The title of the first slide, "Cultural Issues," identified the common denominator of problems. I outlined how the company's culture had crippled effective functioning and reiterated why the NDN was in front of the MPSC:

- Donation process not being maximized

- Underreporting "imminent and eligible" potential donor referrals

- Inadequate hospital development DSA-wide plan and strategy

- Operational performance substandard

- Governance and accountability deficient

I told the MPSC that we had missed out on many heroic donor organ and tissue opportunities and underreported the number of imminent and eligible donor referrals due to poor relationships and faulty process adherence internally and with hospitals in our service area. I also reported that our poor interactions with external local stakeholders, and our weak and broken internal processes, were part of the NDN's deficiencies in governance and accountability protocols, which were far below acceptable guidelines.

I ACKNOWLEDGED OUR ACCOUNTABILITY AND PUT OUR FIRST STAKE IN THE GROUND: ALL THAT, I EMPHASIZED, WAS IN THE PAST.

I acknowledged our accountability and put our first stake in the ground: all that, I emphasized, was in the past.

I quickly moved on to explain where the NDN was in the present—a much better place! That slide, titled "Cultural Transformation," reiterated our new core values of accountability, quality, and excellence (AQE).

I addressed each of the five pillars again, dedicating a slide to each one, with the word **IMPROVED** in bolded all-caps.

We provided three hefty slides of data to support our assertion of improved performance.

The key point we wanted the regulators to focus on was the drastic increase in positive numbers. By July, we'd already experienced a notable rise in viable donor referrals and organs and tissues transplanted

The committee was impressed. But the presentation wasn't over. Merely fixing the broken aspects of the NDN wasn't enough.

After sharing where we were in the past and where we were at the time of the presentation, we wanted to share where we were aiming.

Our final slide stated what and where the NDN planned to be, our new true north: "A world-class organ procurement organization committed to continuous improvement guided by accountability, quality, and excellence to fulfill our mission of saving and improving lives."

After my presentation ended, the team and I braced ourselves for the Q&A.

The questions were rapid fire and directed at me. I learned later we gained favor in the eyes of the committee by having the NDN's leadership answer questions and engage in conversation with the MPSC. That way, it wasn't just me claiming that we were fixing everything. The MPSC heard directly from the leaders who were actively transforming the NDN.

This was very different from the type of engagement the NDN

had practiced in the past, where the strategy was to disagree, deny, or generally act defensively. Instead, the members of the OPTN and the MPSC were hearing something radically different. They were hearing that we owned our dysfunction. Collectively, we were saying, "Yes, this was an issue. This was an area where we failed, and our failure was our fault. This is why it happened; this is how we are fixing it, and here are the results to date."

Shortly after that meeting, I was able to send this email to the NDN: "I am very, very pleased and honored to let you know that after deliberations, the OPTN/UNOS Committee (MPSC) voted unanimously in our favor!!!!! (34 in favor; 0 against; 4 abstentions) The recommendation to remove us as a member has been rescinded!!"

In that email, I took the opportunity to reiterate our true north, adding, "Now that we are moving in the right direction and UNOS is satisfied we are making progress, we can focus on making the Nevada Donor Network the Best OPO in the Nation and the Best Place To Work in this great nation!!!!"

(Yes, there were a lot of exclamation points. It was a big deal! I was excited and wanted the team to share in that excitement.)

A note about true north: It's a maritime navigational term (naturally!) that pilots and boat captains can use as a reference heading to course-correct when currents pull them away from their intended compass heading or bearing. A ship's true course is determined by the direction of the ship relative to a geographic constant known as true north that never changes because it is a straight line toward the geographic North Pole. In leadership terms, it means continuously reviewing metrics and attitudes to ensure alignment to your ultimate goal (direction) as an organization. For a high-performing organization in a tightly regulated industry, optimal compliance and employee engagement includes "true north" indicators. That's the heading we keep an eye on to ensure that if something pulls us away from our course, we are immediately aware and can course-correct, even when there's an adverse event. Everyone makes mistakes, including CEOs. To ensure individuals and organizations don't drift too far off course, it is essential to continually track performance against your true north goals and indicators. The same can also be said for culture.

NO REGRETS

A year after I joined the NDN, an OPO industry colleague asked if I was sick because I looked so radically different from a year before. My first year at the NDN was that intense. I was consumed all the time with nervous energy, never knowing what fresh hell might be awaiting me around the corner. It could be anything from a misappropriated Starbucks gift card to mismanagement of precious, potentially lifesaving organs.

And yet, even if I knew before I started that I would face all of these issues, I still would have taken the job. Even if there were a small part of me that thought fixing the NDN was going to be impossible, I would still have given it my all.

If not, I would have wondered *What if* … for the rest of my life.

Not taking the NDN role would have meant missing out on an opportunity to reach my full potential. Not taking the NDN role meant I wouldn't have gotten my dream job.

My dream job was a nightmare for quite a while. There were lots of times I was worried I wouldn't succeed, and that was pretty nerve-racking.

But if I hadn't taken a chance on running the NDN, with all its attendant risks, then I wouldn't have had the opportunity to make such a difference as part of our team.

CHAPTER 6

BUILDING A SUCCESSFUL INTERNAL CULTURE: TWO STEPS FORWARD, ONE STEP BACK

A s CEO, I initially focused on improving the external perception of the NDN to gain time to make changes that would enable us to function more effectively.

At the same time, there was a lot of internal communication taking place to inspire employee participation in turning the NDN around.

I was clear to everyone that this would be an uncomfortable process! It would involve looking at a tremendous number of mistakes, owning them, and addressing them.

Focusing only on fixing the broken parts wasn't a particularly incentivizing goal. Aiming to become the best OPO in the world or even the universe—a lofty and inconceivable goal for an organization on the brink of being shut down—would be our true north.

When I joined the NDN, employees were reeling. Ensuring their well-being was critical to executing a successful turnaround. My go-to tools were hope and inclusion, and proof that success was possible while practicing transparency, vulnerability, and uncomfortable inclusion as often as required. It reminded me of a quote I shared with the team during the early years by Ernest Hemingway, the Nobel and Pulitzer Prize–winning author who was known for his love of the sea and the human condition: "The world breaks everyone. And afterwards many are stronger in the broken places."

SEEDING HOPE

I immediately began promoting a vision of becoming more than "just" regulatorily compliant and doing an acceptable job.

I wanted everyone at the NDN to know that no matter how bad things were, they were fixable. People needed to understand that participating and contributing to the NDN's true north (to become a world-class organ procurement organization) was a unique opportunity to create something special.

Our transformation began with breaking down silos inside and outside the organization. There was no room for an us-and-them mentality. We were all part of the NDN, and along with the other stakeholders and OPOs in the United States and worldwide, we were all part of a critical, lifesaving, and life-altering mission.

I distributed the DaVita case study to the management team. I asked them to read it, then think about what we could do—as individuals and as a team—to enable a similar seismic change at the NDN.

In sharing the DaVita case studies, I wanted the management team at the NDN to feel hopeful about our vision of success, study and understand the DaVita playbook, and figure out specific actions to effect similar improvements at the NDN.

The case studies helped people see that we were capable of achieving a successful turnaround *if* we were willing to be transparent, vulnerable, accountable, and *committed to changing the culture of the organization.*

Ultimately, my goal was to create belief and hope, to help the organization think, *Hey, here's another company with a new leader that turned a terrible situation around. We can do that too!*

BELIEFS AND BEHAVIORS

For people to have hope, they had to believe in themselves, in me, and in what the NDN was capable of achieving. The DaVita case studies showed that companies in terrible situations could transform by focusing on becoming the best in the world.

While I was writing this book (2020), the NDN was named a Top Workplace by the *Las Vegas Review-Journal.* They awarded us three "culture badges" specific to Innovation, Leaders-in-the-Know, and Open Mindedness. In 2019 we also recorded the world's all-time record for highest donations per capita served, the standard International KPI for all OPOs.

Back in 2012, none of us had any idea of the number of steps—both forward and backward—that it would for us take to get to that point!

Shortly after the team digested the DaVita case studies (and while we were busy creating CAPs and preparing for the July MPSC meeting), I asked the management team to read *Employees First, Customers Second.* Written by Vineet Nayar, the CEO of one of India's leading IT services companies, *Employees First, Customers Second* is a fantastic manual of organizational innovations. *Fortune* magazine described Nayar's leadership as "the world's most modern management."

People in the organization told me that reading *Employees First, Customers Second* was the first time they felt seen and valued. It helped everyone realize that our culture was the source of and solution to our problems.

The book helped set the tone and energy specific to the cultural solutions we needed to implement. Those solutions, based on accountability, quality, and excellence, would help us achieve the goals that would make the NDN a success.

This published success story and transformation did not stop at the staff level. It quickly became apparent that we needed a more diverse board with other leaders to complement the actions of the long-standing board members, who began to drive the change by replacing the CEO with me. So I solicited the help of board members to identify prominent leaders in the community to find successors for them. Several of the board members had served on NDN's board for more than ten years, and even fifteen years in some cases. I knew that we needed more diversity of thought and experience to be a remarkable and unstoppable team. As a matter of fact, we did something that was unheard of in our industry: we solicited high-level experts from outside Nevada, which was a decision that continues to serve us well even today. In most cases in our industry, boards recruit from the local community, and we did that, but we also added talent from other states to complement the locals.

I KNEW THAT WE NEEDED MORE DIVERSITY OF THOUGHT AND EXPERIENCE TO BE A REMARKABLE AND UNSTOPPABLE TEAM.

My close friend Jason, who I met in Miami through my brother many years prior to the NDN while I was still working at the University of Miami, was one such "out-of-state" board member in the initial years. My brother Alex, who is now a successful controller of a large hospital, was working as an assistant controller at the University of Miami hospital reporting to Jason, who was the vice president of finance at the University of Miami hospital. When I lived in South Florida, we fished with family and friends like Jason who shared this passion for boating as often as we could. By 2013 Jason had been the CFO of several hospitals in Florida. Because we did not have anyone on our board at the time with financial expertise and we did not have a full-time CFO, this representation was crucial. I knew enough about finances to be dangerous because of my MBA and leadership positions, but I am no expert like my former CPA boss, Leslie. I knew my place as an operations expert above all else. It was also important for me to recruit people whom I knew and trusted, like Jason, to help us transform at a high level. He accepted a position on our board and traveled once a quarter to Las Vegas for our board meetings and provided the high-level financial knowledge we needed to complement the other board members. After about a year and a half, our annual budget size had nearly doubled from $10 million to $18 million, and I offered him the job as our full-time CFO, which he accepted. He has been an important asset and trusted colleague ever since. Today, our annual budget size is more than $35 million, and we are lucky to have someone of his caliber at the helm of our finances. He also agreed to oversee the human resources component of our organization, which was a critical need. We also recruited transplant surgeons and administrators outside our area to make sure we were overly inclusive in our industry and were inviting diverse points of view, which has proven critical to our success in the long term.

One such high-caliber successor of the longtime board members is a woman named Kathy Silver. One interesting anecdote about her, which she shared with me shortly after we met, was that she actually hemmed Elvis's pants shortly before a performance at the Las Vegas Hotel (LVH), which is now called the Westgate Hotel. When she was growing up in Las Vegas before her incredible career took off, she was working full time at Valley Hospital in the business office and wasn't making enough money to make ends meet, so she took a second job in sales at an exclusive men's store, Cuzzens, which had outlets located in several major hotels. It just so happened that night she was working along with two other girls in the store. Their tailor had gone home for the evening, and the call came in a little later from Elvis's suite. His handlers said he needed his leather pants hemmed for the 8:00 p.m. show. She told them their tailor was already gone, and they panicked (I guess he only had one outfit!). They asked if there wasn't some way that they could make this happen, perhaps by calling back the tailor. She and one of her coworkers realized that you tape leather pants rather than sew them, so they figured for one show they could figure out how to tape them to stay. They then went up to his room, and Elvis was standing on a platform in front of a three-way mirror wearing the pants, and each of them took one leg at a time to tape the pants. He didn't say a word to them, they didn't get a tip, and he wore the pants successfully for both his 8:00 p.m. and midnight shows that night.

She is the former CEO of the University Medical Center in Las Vegas, which is one of the largest county hospitals in the country and has the only transplant program in Nevada. She is currently the president of the Culinary Health Fund in Las Vegas, which represents more than 135,000 covered lives. She's an accomplished healthcare leader born and raised in the Nevada community with a powerful network. Given her passion for transplantation, she made it her priority to support the NDN from a board level. I was very fortunate that she was willing to help, and I did everything I could to show my appreciation and be overly inclusive with her. We had a standing lunch meeting every month, and she helped me understand the Nevada healthcare community. She facilitated contacts and made it her personal goal to make sure our board included at least every major hospital CEO in Nevada. She leveraged her contacts and compelled all of her colleague CEOs of hospitals and associations to be a part of our board. I cannot underscore how crucial this was to our strategy, and I will forever be thankful for her leadership on our behalf. I was lucky that she accepted the chair position of our board one year into my tenure. Thanks to her, our board began to be a formidable force in healthcare in Nevada, and slowly but surely all of the major hospital CEOs were on our board. I would like to think it was because Kathy S. saw the incredible potential of our organization under new leadership as we began to perform and she felt that I was an inclusive leader with potential. Fast-forward to 2020, and even the governor of Nevada, Steve Sisolak, was impressed by the caliber of our board compared to others in our state. We added other members, such as the president and CEO of the Nevada Hospital Association, influential attorneys, a venture capital expert, a CMS/quality improvement expert, and more.

PROVEN PLAYBOOKS

There was no need for us to recreate the wheel. We could leverage countless books, strategic consulting firms, and exercises proven to help management teams practice unity, transparency, and account-ability—and we did! I also knew colleagues in the OPO industry who were very respected and ran high-performing organizations we were striving to become. One such program is the Gift of Life Institute (GOL) in Philadelphia, led by a great friend and mentor named Howard Nathan. Soon after the beginning of our transfor-mation, I traveled to the GOL to meet with Howard and his team. During this trip Howard offered support and guidance, which was invaluable as we began our transformational journey.

My vulnerable solicitation of advice from trusted advisors revealed a common and invaluable theme: when you align beliefs and behaviors, you end up getting results. We aligned our beliefs as a culture—that a transformation based on our true north goal was possible—with our behaviors, which we mapped to our guiding philosophy of accountability, quality, and excellence (AQE).

BELIEFS

BEHAVIORS

Reading the DaVita case studies and *Employees First, Customers Second* was designed to engender hope and belief that a turnaround was possible at the NDN. I also wanted to see how people responded to reading them, which was telling.

It was the people who thought and said, "We can do that too" who became linchpins for the new processes and teams we put into place.

Over time, I got the organization believing in ourselves and adapting behaviors based on an AQE philosophy.

Then we focused on strengthening the three areas that would ensure our success: people, strategy, and systems.

PEOPLE—GETTING THE RIGHT ONES ON BOARD

The initial management survey showed that people felt paralyzed, demoralized, discouraged, and unempowered to effect meaningful change.

Well, we were going to effect meaningful change. That was my message to the team from the beginning. The change was going to start with our organization's DNA, which we were going to reprogram entirely. Our change would revolve around a huge goal: to become the best-performing OPO in the world. The path to that goal would involve fixing the issues that had plagued the organization for years. A popular Latin quote cited throughout history was never more true: *ad astra per aspera,* or "to the stars through difficulty." I shared this quote with our team early on to emphasize that, although things were bleak at the time, we would reach the stars together.

> OUR CHANGE WOULD REVOLVE AROUND A HUGE GOAL: TO BECOME THE BEST-PERFORMING OPO IN THE WORLD.

People who couldn't process significant change either left of their own accord or were exited out. Now that everyone knew what we were trying to do, we would no longer tolerate certain behaviors.

During those first few months, part of the changes that took place involved reassigning or exiting people promoted because of seniority rather than expertise or proven leadership.

We focused on employee health and well-being, being utterly transparent about our large, aspirational goal and how we planned to get there. I stressed that we would always practice uncomfortable inclusion, along with strategic inclusion, involving everyone in creating a new, better, and effective culture.

In creating the right kind of culture, you need the right kind of people on board. This was an area where I made some big mistakes. After the MPSC rescinded our "Member Not in Good Standing" status, it was easier to hire people from the OPO industry.

Instead of practicing inclusivity, I rushed forward and hired people on my own. I knew the type of experienced hires I wanted, and I didn't consult with other people in the organization. I hired people based solely on their résumés instead of their personalities. After a year or so, I had to exit most of the new hires I'd made. They had the right OPO experience—that's why I had hired them—but they didn't have the right mindset for the culture we were building at the NDN.

Each time our dramatic growth required support, I'd regress and start a solo hiring spree. I'd hire too many people, too quickly, without input from others. I forgot one of my other favorite Peter Drucker quotes: "When you hire a hand, they come with a heart and mind attached." I was hiring bodies and brains, not personalities. That was a mistake. I finally learned my lesson about our hiring practices (described in more detail later on in the chapter). Not one of the new management hires I made early on in that first wave is still with the NDN today.

Our culture wasn't something we could simply announce. It took time to identify and evolve and become meaningful. We had to hire people who understood the value of transparency and were open to making mistakes and learning from them.

Our management team also read Jim Collins's book *Good to Great*. What resonates most is that all great companies evolve over time. Great companies go through iterative processes and aren't afraid to blow something up if it isn't working. They go through phases of invention and reinvention, looking critically at each new path to see if it works. If it isn't working, they fix it. We adopted and practiced that mindset at the NDN. It took time.

The way I was hiring people didn't work. We fixed it, first by bringing in more people from across the organization to consider new hires from a cultural-fit perspective.

In the next chapter, I'll discuss our inclusive hiring practices and how they are a cornerstone of our culture and success at the NDN. In short, today, regardless of the seniority of the role or area of responsibility, every new hire at the NDN must meet with a certain number of people in the organization who evaluate them *solely based on their prospective cultural fit.*

That strategy, integral to our success, has nearly tripled our employee numbers and is a direct offshoot of the original hiring mistakes I made.

STRATEGY—FULL EMPLOYEE ENGAGEMENT

At many organizations, the strategy is determined and designed by a small number of people in executive management, then distributed as writ throughout the organization. For organizations with tens of thousands of employees, that makes sense. For smaller organizations, where every person contributes to a thriving culture and facilitates effective operations, there's a lot of value in involving everyone in strategy discussions.

Make no mistake: doing so is messy and hard. It might seem unnecessarily difficult, complicated, and uncomfortable. We decided early on to involve all employees in creating the NDN strategy for success. That proved to be the right choice for us.

It did start at the top. The accountability, quality, and excellence philosophy was something I strongly recommended to our executive team that we adopt and follow. In a presentation to the entire company, I shared how adhering to AQE helped the executive team create and sustain CAPs, which were crucial in convincing the MPSC we were on the right path.

One way to maximize the potential of a team is to bring everyone behind the curtain to understand the reasons behind adopting a new strategy. Doing so helps engender a similar mindset. Once everyone saw how AQE effected change, they practiced that mindset. From that point forward we enabled everyone in the organization to contribute strategically to solving challenges and focusing on our true north.

Bottom-Up Strategic Planning: SWOT

Prior to 2012, the NDN team had never participated in strategic planning as a group. The previous administration would hand them timelines, budgets, and operational targets to hit without their input. No wonder everyone felt so disconnected and helpless.

Preparing for the MPSC meeting marked the first time the management team provided input about the NDN's direction. They were active in designing CAPs that acknowledged our accountability for failures and, more rewardingly, in creating plans designed to elevate the NDN to new heights.

Like my former boss, Leslie, did for me, I asked department leaders to prepare individual and team strengths, weaknesses, opportunities, threats (SWOT) analysis documents with aspirational goals for the short term (a year) and long term (to make the NDN a world-leading OPO over time). Then I asked everyone in the organization to work on a SWOT analysis for the entire organization based on their observations.

Organizations often hesitate to do something like this—invite company-wide feedback as part of a major fix—because it is uncomfortable. Understandably, leaders often say to their executive team, "OK, put a plan in place, and tell your staff to accomplish it," rather than making the entire workforce part of the planning and execution process with maximum inclusion.

It is definitely more work to include a huge number of people in strategic analysis and planning. The first time we did, it was messy and complicated. Over time, our bottom-up strategic planning evolved into the sophisticated process we practice today. Department heads involve their entire staff in an initial SWOT analysis. Together, they determine agreed-upon goals they're responsible for and design strategies and tactics to facilitate success, which are aligned with the overall objectives of the organization. As a result of this uncomfortable inclusion, the buy-in is unmatched.

By involving the entire organization in reviewing itself, we reinforce synergy, cooperation, and unity while cultivating better ideas and innovation. It is critical to include everyone, because ultimately the frontline staff knows best what their environment is going to look like tomorrow and likely a few years down the line, and they are best positioned to be innovators. Why wouldn't we have them as part of the planning process?

Uncomfortable Inclusion for Everyone!

Uncomfortable inclusion means being transparent (inclusive) to the point of discomfort, like we were in 2012 in front of the MPSC. I still believe that if it is not uncomfortable, you are not being inclusive enough.

When leaders are inclusive at all levels, they help build a cultural and operational infrastructure where everyone influences decision-making and innovation. Inclusion—uncomfortable or otherwise—leads to what I call decision equity or decision capital.

UNCOMFORTABLE INCLUSION MEANS BEING TRANSPARENT (INCLUSIVE) TO THE POINT OF DISCOMFORT.

When you're transparent with team members and include them in decision-making, you create a network of stakeholders who participate even in small decisions. When it comes time to make more impactful decisions, a leader can tap into that banked brain trust to make the best decision possible based on feedback from a proven set of deciders.

I did not know how powerful decision capital would be at the time I joined the NDN. It evolved naturally from our practice of uncomfortable inclusion and became an integral part of our culture.

It's always hard for people to hear that they aren't doing a good job, so there's a natural tendency to be defensive and sugarcoat things, both as the deliverer of that information and as the recipient.

Upending that tendency is painful and necessary. Practicing uncomfortable inclusion as a collective process made it easier for everyone. We were all being transparent and taking responsibility for decisions made in a previously toxic environment. Singling out individuals to blame wasn't the point and didn't happen. We even engaged with our most vocal critics! In my view, our critics and antagonists are the most important catalysts for growth and innovation.

This idea of our enemies being crucial to our growth reminds me of a somewhat apocryphal tale about an early-twentieth-century experiment involving cod and catfish. I note its confusing origins because the first time I presented this story at a conference plenary, an experienced fisherman came up afterward to tell me that my descriptions of geography and ichthyology weren't entirely correct. However, the meaning of the tale is highly relevant, and you can find multiple versions of it online and in business books.

It goes something like this: In the early 1900s the demand for cod on the east coast remained high, while east coast pools of cod were shrinking due to overfishing. Entrepreneurs tried different methods of shipping cod from the west coast to the east coast but with little success in delivering a usable product. Even shipping live fish in tanks resulted in cod arriving on the east coast sickly and lethargic, unfit for eating. Someone came up with the idea of placing one of the natural enemies of the cod—catfish—in the tanks. The catfish would chase the cod around, keeping them lively and active, simulating a natural, in-the-wild environment up until the cod arrived on the east coast. The logic behind the idea was that fish kept constantly on alert against threats and competition for food kept them competitive, viable, and healthy. The experiment worked! I find this anecdote to be a valuable business learning and tool, illustrating that complacency and isolation (similar to the state of mind that helped lead the Nevada Donor Network to the brink of demise) is never a healthy environment for any living organism. Our loudest critics and competitors are the best sources of this necessary stimulus for organizational vitality.

In 2015, the NDN was invited by our loudest critic, the OPTN/UNOS, to present a webinar about our practice of accountability. Accountability is all about uncomfortable inclusion because you have to self-report a mistake, as painful as that might be, explain how the mistake happened, why it happened, what steps you are taking to fix it, and the metrics you have in place to measure your corrective plan's efficacy.

That presentation included a major adverse event from earlier that year that became the focal point of our accountability presentation. Rather than feel ashamed or embarrassed, we took the opportunity to show how that proactive self-reporting and self-correction allowed us to put steps in place to ensure a similar adverse event never happened again.

An Adverse Event and Accountability

It was the most calamitous issue to occur during our renaissance, a few years after MPSC removed us from the watch list. It also provided a solid opportunity for the NDN to demonstrate our evolved communication and operational practices.

In 2015 the NDN handled a number of kidney and tissue recoveries and transports, given that 90 percent of the organs recovered locally are exported for transplantation in other states by NDN. Nonetheless each one was a big deal. There's always a huge waiting list of critical patients who need healthy kidneys, so this is precious cargo.

In one twenty-four-hour period, we recovered kidneys from two heroic donors. A potential recipient was scheduled to receive a kidney, and the tissues were going to a kidney processor.

There's a necessarily complex checking system for the pickup and transport of organs or tissues intended for transplantation or for further processing. The labeling itself is sophisticated and details the parameters of transport, as well as what is being transported. Given the stakes, verification of information in and on the package is critical.

Some of the clinical staff at the NDN would not stay on-site after they packaged organs or tissues for transport to the transplanting center or tissue processor, respectively. Instead, they would leave the package in designated areas in our multiple buildings, open twenty-four hours, for pickup by specialized courier services. The NDN staff in these twenty-four-hour pickup areas were not always clinicians. Because we had not refined our process and trained them properly, they didn't know how to interpret the labeling system and would simply hand the boxes over to the courier service. The courier service wasn't responsible for checking the boxes' contents. That was the job of the OPO or tissue bank and, thankfully, the receiving hospital, lab, or tissue processor, as applicable.

The transplant hospital received the box of tissue grafts instead of the kidney for their waiting potential recipient. They caught the error. It took an extra amount of time to reroute the correct package containing the kidney to the hospital, and the longer transport time could have ultimately impacted its optimal viability and the clinical outcome of the recipient. In short, the extended transport time for the kidney was unnecessary and dangerous for the recipient. Our carelessness also dishonored the heroic donor and their family. Fortunately, the kidney was transplanted and the recipient did well.

However, our failure in this situation was egregious.

We immediately self-reported this massive error to the OPTN safety portal. We convened a rapid-response team to contain the issue and ensure this would not happen again during cases in the following days. Then we performed a root-cause analysis to determine how this had happened. We put a corrective action plan in place to prevent a similar issue from ever happening again by refining our process and training the team properly. And we determined packaging and shipping guidelines and audits to be checked and met as part of the ongoing adherence to an improved protocol until the new process stabilized.

For some time early on in our transformation, I even participated as the clinical administrator on call until I could help get the right process and the right team of people in place. I personally participated in organ recovery cases and helped monitor packing processes to verify accuracy—while running the organization!

Here's how we presented our experience to the OPO industry.

We provided context, acknowledging the legacy culture issues that had led to sloppy internal procedures, which hampered effective oversight. We shared how adhering to an AQE philosophy strengthened the NDN's commitment to aligning our behaviors with our true north goal. Adhering to true north required having active vigilance and monitoring systems in place to catch variances (too much variance was usually a sign that something was off). We talked about the process we had in place for when an adverse event occurred, which is to perform a root-cause analysis (RCA)—beyond just saying, "Our culture sucked, and no one wanted to speak up"—and, based on what the RCA showed, design an effective CAP. Finally, we shared the establishment of an internal quality assurance and performance improvement council (QAPI), a stand-alone team focused solely on helping managers map their plans to the highest quality standards as set forth by the OPTN/UNOS.

ADVERSE EVENT

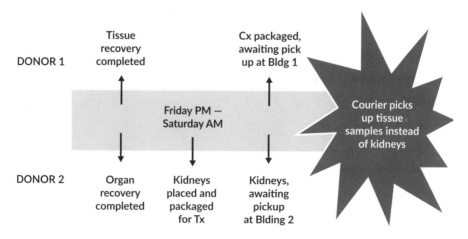

PROBLEM

Tissue culture picked up first, sent to TXC instead of kidneys

Mistake realized when package received at TXC and box was opened

Courier dispatched immediately, picked up kidneys and drove to TXC

Kidneys transplanted several hours later with increased cold ischemia time

ROOT-CAUSE ANALYSIS

No centralized place for shipment pickup

Coordinator delivered kidneys to office with later pickup by courier

No system/SOP to verify package picked up and delivery

Traveling Coordinator staff

High donation volumes with limited staff

CORRECTIVE ACTION

Requires a "time-out" verification of contents and destination before hand-off

Verification of process documented on packing slip provided by courier

Staff trained on procedure before any hand-offs to courier

More full-time experienced staff hired (common theme)

HIGHLIGHTS OF SOLUTION

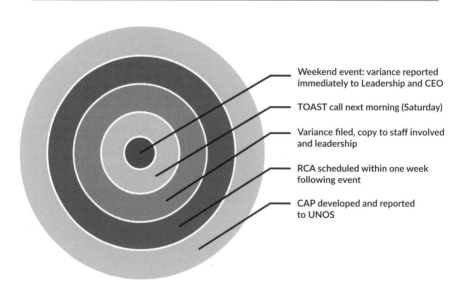

Weekend event: variance reported immediately to Leadership and CEO

TOAST call next morning (Saturday)

Variance filed, copy to staff involved and leadership

RCA scheduled within one week following event

CAP developed and reported to UNOS

That final slide showed how much work we had done internally to create effective systems to support our evolving culture.

SYSTEMS—SUPPORTING THE TEAM

Some of the systems we put in place—practicing a root-cause analysis of issues, promoting transparency about causes, and implementing metrics-based fixes—were simply a matter of adapting proven management systems specific to the NDN's standards for success. The management team essentially went through a mini-MBA course through our reading materials, exercises, utilization of strategic consultants, and thoughtfully designed management retreats.

In the final slide detailing the kidney mix-up, we showed how our system enabled us to conduct rapid reviews, fixes, monitoring metrics, and communication to the OPTN/UNOS in the case of an adverse event.

- The Variance (error) was immediately reported to the leadership team (including me). This was established as SOP at the NDN shortly after my arrival to lend transparency without the fear of retribution to the process.

- We held a TOAST (Tissue Organ/Ocular Activity Summary Teleconference) to review what happened. (The NDN now holds TOASTS twice daily for the purpose of communicating the day's pending activity among the various departments.)

- The details of the adverse event were confirmed and officially logged, within the organization and with the OPTN/UNOS.

- The team conducted an immediate RCA (root-cause analysis) and provided documentation detailing what led to the adverse event.

- The RCA, coupled with a CAP to prevent future similar adverse events, was shared with the OPTN/UNOS as a follow-up to our initial self-reporting.

At the NDN, we established quality as a goal and true north. By making the practice of self-reporting errors of any kind routine, adherence to quality became an ongoing behavior rather than a measurement to illustrate failures.

In our accountability presentation, we shared how self-reporting errors improved our credibility as an organization. This process of self-reporting is something that we still do today, no matter how uncomfortable or unfortunate. We recently had another impactful opportunity to practice accountability and self-reporting, which I'll describe in the next chapter.

The NDN is a complex organization operating in a highly regulated space. The systems we put in place were rarely successful the first time out of the gate. We had to try a few different ways of doing things, fail, step back, restrategize, and try again. And again. And again.

RELENTLESS REFERRAL MANAGEMENT, INCREASED CAPACITY, TECHNOLOGY, AND DATA

In my two decades of working in the OPO space, I've learned that for an OPO to be as productive and successful as possible, it must have a relentless referral management process. When a hospital picks up the phone and calls the OPO to say they have a potential donor, the OPO team must be *immediately* responsive. Expeditious and thorough responses ensure an optimum donor process.

Immediacy is key: if a heroic donor's gifts (a single heroic organ donor can provide up to nine life-changing transplants and up to seventy-five or more tissues) are to have the maximum impact, an OPO must respond to, manage, recover, and transport those organs and tissues as soon as possible. I had a ton of clinical expertise in this area from my time at the University of Miami's OPO.

When I got to the NDN, I discovered that the systems we had in place were responsible for our poor track record, given how siloed the processes were. If a hospital called the NDN after standard working hours with notification of a potential donor, rather than having a trained OPO professional at that hospital within the hour, we would instead defer seeing the potential donor until the next morning. This was not due to laziness or disinterest but to poor staffing decisions. A previous manager had determined that it didn't make budgetary sense to have staff manage donor referrals during the night, thinking the day shift would handle the few calls that came in after hours. Unfortunately, the day-shift staff was overloaded with activity during the day, which compromised the opportunity to follow up on calls received the night before, focusing instead on the calls about potential donors that came in during the day. Oftentimes the patient's status would change overnight, and by the time the day shift followed up, donation opportunities were compromised or even lost. This behavior was immediately changed.

An important aspect of our philosophy and ultimate success in this area focused on minimizing the burden of the hospital staff's referral process. The nurses and doctors who call potential donor referrals to an OPO are often busy taking care of several patients. To make it easier for them, we decided we would be überresponsive and show up in person right away, even if the likelihood of donation was low, so they didn't have to spend extra time on the phone with us.

The change in our donor referral pursuance policy to be relentless and diligent was something I learned from my time at the University of Miami, which meant we were more present and active as quickly as possible after receiving a call about a potential heroic donor. Expanding our availability meant hiring experienced personnel to handle different types of potential donor evaluations and conversations. That investment in system resources (specifically, people) increased our capacity to reach more potential donors faster and obtain more exceptional results, especially related to organ viability and authorization for donation. Reflecting back on my failed management of the post-hurricane business venture after high school with a blown transmission by not considering the limitations of my resources, this investment in people was key to make sure we didn't burn people out with the increased activity. We also invested in an internal technology program known as iTransplant (provided by Transplant Connect) early on as our donor referral information system that frequently monitored cumulative donor referral data, and our linked performance scorecard would immediately alert us if a significant variance indicated a need for our attention. To accomplish this we set thresholds for evaluation on our metrics, which meant that when a referral indicator at a hospital rose or fell by a certain amount, it would be evaluated for action by our team. This would allow for efficiency in goal management.

This system had become so advanced in 2019 since we invested in it years ago that it can now plug into the hospital's electronic medical records and automatically alert our team of a potential donor based on certain clinical triggers or allow for push-button notification by the nurse or doctor with little to no effort. We believe this is the future of our industry. Transplant Connect's visionary founder and CEO, John Piano, developed this capability, known as iReferral, to try to facilitate a more seamless way for electronic notification of donor referrals by the hospital personnel rather than the time-consuming phone process. At NDN we were one of the first testers and early adopters of this technology in collaboration with Transplant Connect, and today it has become a great contributor to donor referral management, which can sometimes be a great burden to very busy hospital staff members, as discussed earlier.

Modeled after the process utilized by the University of Miami OPO during my days there, we also implemented a daily reporting function of active donor cases and referrals in use today at the NDN called TOAST that I'll describe in more detail in the next chapter.

The upshot of all the incredible work we did during 2012 and 2013 resulted in these outcomes:

- June 2013: The OPTN/UNOS restored the Nevada Donor Network to Full Membership status. The president of the OPTN/UNOS said, "The organization is to be commended for its noticeable improvement in the vital services it provides for donor families and candidates awaiting transplantation." We were declared fully CMS compliant in 2013 and regained our AOPO accreditation in May 2014.

- May 2013: The Nevada Donor Network announced[5] record-breaking increases in all aspects of organ and tissue donation, noting that "improvements in our operational systems for capturing donation potential in collaboration with our hospital partners has been a marked success."

The new people, strategies, and systems we put in place appeared to be working.

But appearances aren't always 100 percent reflective of reality.

---

5   "Nevada Donor Network Announces Unprecedented Growth in Organ & Tissue Donation," CISION PR Newswire, press release, May 16, 2013, https://www.prnewswire.com/news-releases/nevada-donor-net-work-announces-unprecedented-growth-in-organ--tissue-donation-207726581.html.

CHAPTER 7

EYES WIDE SHUT

Regaining credibility and significantly increasing our productivity had not gone unnoticed within our industry, which helped as we began to recruit after the second management purge (the lesson where I learned to be more inclusive in the hiring process). We were no longer dismissed as a poorly performing entity, and our peers often recognized our innovations and success.

In May of 2013, we were able to announce unprecedented growth in organ and tissue donation. Our success, detailed in a press release, received notice nationally in the *Wall Street Journal* and other major regional publications:

> Also driving Nevada Donor Network's growth is our increasing organ donation authorization rate, which rose from 48% in early 2012 to 69% by the end of the year. During the first quarter of 2013, the authorization rate continued to rise to an all-time high of 82%.
>
> Nevada Donor Network President and Chief Executive Officer Joseph Ferreira says the growth can be attributed to a number of factors. "An overall improvement in the attitudes regarding donation in the community,

coupled with improvements in our operational systems for capturing donation potential in collaboration with our hospital partners has been a marked success. I am very proud of our team, hospital partners and community advocates who have helped contribute to such a successful year of meaningful change with so many lives saved and improved."

A year after I joined the NDN, we hired a PR and marketing firm to increase awareness of our organization and updated our brand. (In fact, a local transplant recipient designed our new logo!)

The logo depicts a person made of an infinity sign, signifying that life continues thanks to donation and transplantation

In June 2013, I got to participate in a great Q&A with our local paper, the *Las Vegas Review-Journal*, which wrote about our improved numbers and our ongoing commitment to continuous improvement:

In the short time Ferreira has overseen the procurement network, he has unquestionably contributed to the following figures: From 2011 through 2012, the number of transplanted intestines jumped 400 percent, kidney procurement increased by 30 percent and the number of transplanted livers jumped 24 percent. "We are performing better as an organization than we have ever performed in our history," Ferreira said. Although the statistics are impressive, Ferreira acknowledges he and the organization still have potential for improvement.

We were publicly committing to our culture of inclusion, transparency, and open communication. As a result, our metrics across the board were improving.

RELATIONSHIP RESTORATION AND VALUE-ADD

Our improved numbers stemmed from the investment we made in improving our relationships with external stakeholders along with investments in our team. To get to that point, we took a hard look at our existing poor relationships to figure out what to improve.

We focused on the following:

- **Benchmarking our performance against high performers.** This was the peer group we wanted not only to be a part of but to lead!

- **Restoration of relationships with community partners.** We had a lot of work to do to regain the trust and cooperation from local hospitals and other support organizations we relied upon to learn of potential heroic donors.

- **Value-add to our community partners.** We couldn't just ask for a better relationship with our local partners; we had to inspire it by being a fantastic partner ourselves. A great example is our current relationship with the coroner's office in Las Vegas that I'll describe further on in the chapter.

- **Entrepreneurial-spirit approach.** This was another mindset I focused on fostering internally, encouraging people to take a leadership approach and think of creative solutions specific to their remit. I led by example, using several resources (such as the books and consulting groups) that helped people understand what it meant to embody and practice an entrepreneurial spirit. In short, it meant taking ownership and thinking of creative solutions based on similar successes in the business world. This is an area where many nonprofits miss the boat by not using proven playbooks perfected at entrepreneurial companies. Our entrepreneurial efforts came to fruition in 2019, with the launch of an innovative relationship that adds value to our tissue donation and transplantation ecosystem in the US and the Australian community. I'll discuss that initiative later in the chapter.

LISTEN TO YOUR DOCTOR AND NURSE

My OPO experience in Miami was uniquely beneficial in fostering better communication between OPO and transplant teams at hospitals nationwide.

In the donation/transplant community, there can be a tense or combative relationship between the OPOs and the transplant teams. Donation teams sometimes think transplant surgeons aren't sensitive enough to what the donor family or the donor hospital staff is experiencing. That's not the case. Transplant doctors and nurses are aware of delicate procurement dynamics. Primarily, they are laser-focused on saving a critical patient who needs a transplant to survive. They balance honoring a heroic donor and their family while engaging in a time-critical fight to save their patient's life.

At the University of Miami's OPO, I worked closely with transplant surgeons and nurse coordinators to understand their mindset. I had a very healthy appreciation and respect for the needs of the transplant staff. I knew from personal experience that when an OPO collaborates with a transplant team, the outcomes are always better. I brought this mindset with me to the NDN.

At that time, we exported 90 percent of the organs and tissues we recovered to centers across the country. To be successful, we needed to become *extremely* accommodating and useful to regional and national teams who, to date, had little respect for patience to work with the NDN. The organization's slowness and sloppiness in providing crucial details transplant surgeons needed to make informed decisions about whether or not to transport an organ meant transplant surgeons across the United States loathed getting organ offers from the NDN. These decision makers routinely charter private planes to secure a healthy donor gift. They learned not to assign tremendous resources based on information from the NDN, which frequently was insufficient or outdated (which can happen rapidly when information changes by the hour). We had to change that.

I encouraged the NDN team to practice awareness of the complicated and critical situations facing transplant surgeons and teams. They began actively listening to surgeons' needs and figuring out how we could be of the most help to them and their elaborate teams.

As a result of hearing what transplant teams wanted and needed, we first focused on improving our "rule in, rule out" decisions.

The doctors on staff at the NDN were not typically transplant surgeons, and even if they were, they frequently would "rule out" organs and tissues based on generic guidelines. This practice vastly limits the supply of potentially lifesaving organs and tissues at any given time. If the transplant teams never hear about a potential donor that is ruled out by the OPO team, donation and transplantation does not happen.

Transplant surgeons tend not to rule out any donor organ for patients who are critical as a hard-and-fast rule. There's a great book by Thomas Starzl called *The Puzzle,* which explains transplant surgeons' decision-making process in great detail. They are under immense pressure to save lives and need to be creative in mixing and matching recipients with the best organ or tissues available at that moment.

Giving transplant surgeons all the relevant information of a donor and organ, even if it doesn't fit a standard template of what's viable, ensures they can make an informed decision on behalf of their patient for themselves.

We began cultivating a practice of moving mountains for transplant surgeons and teams, even if it took a toll on us. That's a customer-service-based philosophy that I learned at the University of Miami's OPO from transplant surgeons who trained with Thomas Starzl and other giants in the industry.

The best practice, we determined, was for the NDN not to make decisions on behalf of the surgeons who were transplanting the organs. Rather, our role was transparently and comprehensively telling the story of the heroic potential donor referral and the family to allow the transplant surgeons to decide viability.

We became precise storytellers, committed to sharing every possible relevant facet of a potential donor's history.

We'd make offers to transplant centers all over the country because one doctor may be more willing than another to accept a specific organ or tissue. We could only determine this if we resisted the urge to rule things out early on based on likelihood of acceptance, which is a common mistake some OPOs make.

Making our culture more inclusive with the transplant teams who make these decisions, no matter how uncomfortable, vastly increased the number and utility of donor gifts. It takes a lot of time and energy for us to deliver on going that extra mile consistently. But doing so is part of our true north.

For example, a young woman was placed on life support after being found unresponsive due to a drug overdose in a hotel room. A few days after receiving her as a potential donor referral she was declared brain dead by hospital physicians. She had no immediately apparent family in town. Moreover, her work as a prostitute and her drug overdose made her a nonstandard, high-risk donor.

We knew some transplant surgeons would be willing to consider her gifts due to her relatively young age and lack of disease or damage due to drug use. However, she needed someone to give permission for her to be a heroic donor because she was not registered as a donor. The NDN took the lead on finding her family, who had lost touch with her, given her lifestyle choices.

It took an immense amount of time and effort over several days in order to track down her family to let them know of her grave prognosis and ask them for authorization so that she could become a heroic donor. Thanks to NDN's efforts, the family had the opportunity to learn of what had happened to their estranged daughter, say goodbye, and give their permission to change the lives of recipients nationwide who benefited from her gifts. Had we not invested the time and energy to finding them and "ruled her out" as a potential donor, their loved one would have died alone, and several other people who received her precious organs would not be alive today. Prior to our transformation, this young woman's case may not have been pursued by the staff. Now that we had changed our mindset to be relentless on behalf of the heroic donor, their courageous families, and the desperate recipients, we were saving more lives, and more donor families had solace knowing their loved one left a legacy of life no matter how tragic the circumstances were.

ENTREPRENEURIAL MINDSET

In addition to improving the utility of donor gifts, over time we also increased the availability of heroic donor gifts themselves. (That isn't as concerning as it might sound.)

It's the result of *thinking creatively in pursuit of our true north, for the NDN to be a world-class organ procurement organization committed to continuous improvement guided by accountability, quality, and excellence to fulfill our mission of saving and improving lives.*

Many people don't die in a hospital, so partnering with "out-of-hospital" entities increases our referral network and our insight into available potential donors. In turn, that increases our value to waiting organ and tissue recipients worldwide.

We've expanded our local relationships with law enforcement, medical examiners, and coroners to include them in our referral network to ensure all heroic donors are identified, no matter where they pass away.

In the early years after we more closely partnered with the Clark County coroner, Dr. Michael P. Murphy, and the assistant coroner, John Fudenberg, along with the medical examiners on staff (we even occupy space in the coroner's office to streamline donor recoveries), that relationship immediately became the largest source of tissue and ocular donor referrals. When Dr. Murphy retired, John became the coroner and continued to be a fantastic partner to NDN.

Hospitals routinely take a blood sample from people admitted due to a traumatic event (such as a car crash). If relevant, they may test blood samples for toxic substances. They discard the admission blood sample a few days after admission or if the person dies. Medical examiners are the ones responsible for determining the exact cause and manner of death. They want and need to test an admission blood sample for toxic substances, but by the time the ME is involved, the hospitals have already discarded it in many cases.

The NDN has access to admission blood samples for all traumatic cases of people who could be prospective heroic donors in order to evaluate them for donation at the appropriate time. We told the coroner's office we would save admission blood samples for them. That way, if a person died, the ME could get the admission blood sample and run toxicology tests to inform their final report on the cause of death. We also committed to facilitating scans and further testing if a deceased donor was authorized for donation and under our care to help MEs make an informed decision about what happened to the victim prior to death. It's all part of our mission to be a positive partner and a good member of the overall ecosystem of individuals who help advance the OPO mission. Our mindset has been that their mission of finding the cause and manner of death to be the voice of the victim is just as important as ours of saving lives, and we treat it as such. The local coroner and MEs are grateful for our help and presence and are vigilant in alerting us of potential life-changing organ and tissue donation opportunities from recently deceased individuals. Our willingness to go above and beyond for them was a great example of our mindset to be value additive to their critical mission rather than just ask them for help with our mission. Within three years of focusing on these mutually value-added partnerships, the number of our tissue donors grew by 300 percent.

Our process of maximum inclusion and collaboration with out-of-hospital community partners, donor hospitals, and transplant teams increased our value to the entire organ and tissue transplant ecosystem worldwide, now that it was clear we wanted them to succeed in their mission just as much as we wanted to succeed. It even led to an opportunity to help diverse communities all over the world in a meaningful way.

A serendipitous seating arrangement led to a very cool and unique international joint venture between the NDN and an Australian biotechnology company. One of our directors attended a conference (the American Association of Tissue Banks) and sat next to an Australian tissue recovery agency representative. Australia's donation and authorization rates are challenged, so the representative was in the United States looking for opportunities to access donor tissue from this country.

One part of the donor recovery and transport system is the procurement and processing of viable tissues for implantation. There are specific gifts—bone, skin, and musculoskeletal tissues—refined into grafts for patients who need ACL repairs, heart valve replacements, or skin grafts.

The lovely Australian woman, named Sharon, at the conference worked for a tissue processor in Australia that was looking for more heroic donor tissues from the United States, given their lack of supply, to help people in need in her home country.

What our director of tissue services at the time thought was that there was an opportunity for the NDN to partner with the Australian processing company as an outlet for heroic donor tissues that are not accepted for implantation in the US. Such a partnership could be mutually beneficial; it would bring processing power to Nevada to benefit patients in the United States and increase tissue availability for Australian recipients. It was an intriguing idea to set up a new type of relationship that could advance international cooperation in this area. Going into this potential relationship, I committed to the high-performing, visionary CEO named Simon Berry of the Australian processor that we would only do this if there could be a clear benefit to them and their country. We wanted to help increase donation in Australia so that they could be successful and not just benefit the NDN in the US.

No one had thought of setting up an international relationship like this before with Australia, probably (in part) because the regulatory hurdles of sharing tissues between two countries are extraordinarily complex, crossing several regulatory agencies. For example, we started thinking about the idea of a joint venture tissue-processing partnership between Las Vegas and Sydney, Australia, in 2014. The donor-sharing component with Australia finally came to fruition in 2016, and the donor processing facility in Las Vegas began operations in 2019, the result of years of hard work and entrepreneurial "What if we tried this?" thinking.

One of my favorite proponents of the entrepreneurial mindset in the nonprofit world is Dan Pallotta (https://www.danpallotta.com/), a wildly successful entrepreneur who advocates that more nonprofits need to act like successful for-profit companies if they presume to dream big to solve the complex and widespread social issues they confront. He terms these concepts *social innovation* and *entrepreneurship*. Through the case studies and business books we read as a management team and what I learned during my MBA curriculum, these concepts are clearly successful in private businesses and publicly traded companies. To be clear, incorporating these business strategies doesn't mean the executives are driven by profiteering or getting personal shares or are individually inured by donation activities at OPOs. As a matter of fact, that is against the law and OPO policies. Like all other nonprofits, executive compensation is decided by the board through market analysis and compensation studies for other executives in nonprofits all over the country. Our mission at the NDN is a clinical and social one at its very core, and any profiteering by its employees would compromise trust and integrity in the system. At the same time, people's lives depend on our ability to perform well. Consequently, we should be well funded, attract and retain the top talent while paying them comparatively well, and take calculated risks on initiatives for a maximum return on behalf of those we honor and serve in donation and transplantation. These concepts have reverberated so much in our culture at NDN that we asked Dan Pallotta to speak to our executive team and board in 2018 at a strategic retreat held annually. His message resonated with our board members and executive team because it brought to life what we had been doing to save and heal as many lives as possible. This discipline has ensured that our entrepreneurial mindset is supported and celebrated throughout the organization, including at the board level. After all, if the board members and the highest ranks do not support the entrepreneurial spirit, it is challenging to sustain among the team and innovate along the way. My third board chair during my tenure, Dr. Trudy Larson, is an incredibly accomplished infectious disease physician and community leader. Among other things, she has been a primary catalyst at the board level to help drive our entrepreneurial spirit by supporting this mentality and mindset, which resulted in this meeting with Dan and several great initiatives because of her leadership. This was a pivotal meeting to strive for the next level of success.

The value is not only to individual patients but also to increase awareness worldwide of best practices for facilitating donations. Our relationship with the biotechnology company in Australia resulted in people coming to the United States from several countries to learn our protocols and export them back home, to increase awareness around donation and procurement techniques, and to improve utilization and acceptance of donations.

Back in Nevada, the benefits were multifold. We started the

tissue processor in Las Vegas with our partner, which created more jobs locally and benefited patients in Nevada who needed tissues. It also allows us to keep more of these precious gifts in our local community, but more importantly, it allows us to be involved in all aspects of the heroic donation process, including the processing of tissues. Any proceeds to NDN from these activities are always reinvested into the organization for the benefit of the community and the mission we serve. There is no doubt that this collaborative mindset has contributed to our high performance by facilitating unique interactions and resources to propel our mission forward through both social and financial investment in our team.

Our industry-changing investment now has international accreditation and is considered the gold standard of how international cooperation can save and improve lives worldwide thanks to the heroic donors.

Since 2014, we've increased our processing partners from two to seven (for different types of donor tissues and grafts that have varying degrees of acceptance criteria based on the various contracts and demand for tissue in the implanting hospitals, dentists' offices, and surgery centers) to maximize donation opportunities by mutually beneficial relationships.

We constantly evaluate our partner mix to identify gaps and maximize new opportunities to recover more gifts from more donors. In 2019 we launched a Birth Tissue Donation program that lets mothers choose to donate birth tissue that can heal wounds for diabetic patients and provide stem cells for research and regenerative applications. Only a few OPOs offer this type of program, and we are at the forefront of this new and exciting service to the community. The most remarkable part about this offering is that we now not only serve the heroic donors upon death in a tragic circumstance by courageous families, but we are now are able to offer hope, strength, and life when a new soul is brought into this world during the happiest of times for a family.

Our diversified and entrepreneurial strategy means we now have multiple outlets to access and utilize heroic donors' gifts, all in the interest of helping more people through the gift of donation.

> **YOU CAN'T OVERESTIMATE THE INSPIRATION AND POWER THAT COMES FROM INCLUDING PEOPLE (TO THE POINT OF DISCOMFORT) WITHIN THE ORGANIZATION.**

Innovative growth and development ideas come from our practice of being receptive to different perspectives from all parts of the organization and beyond. You can't overestimate the inspiration and power that comes from including people (to the point of discomfort) within the organization while also making sure our organization benefits from external partner inclusion by ensuring there is a value-add for them to partner with your team.

EYES WIDE OPEN

In 2019 the NDN was swinging right along in smooth waters and a following sea.

We were hiring the right people and exceeding our numbers year after year. We were leveraging every opportunity to increase our value to our concentric community circles locally, nationally, and internationally. For six years straight, the NDN was recognized as the world's top-performing OPO. We were knocking it out of the park.

Then came a brutal reminder of a storm that no matter how quickly you can grow, it is imperative not to lose sight of the values and guiding philosophy.

We had a solid track record of hiring better people and infusing the organization with increased adherence to quality. We continued to break records across the board. But our infrastructure and quality processes couldn't keep pace with our growth. Focusing on breaking records while establishing comprehensive quality controls for our rapidly growing organization was like trying to change a propellor on an accelerating boat.

The eye bank of the NDN was one such accelerating boat. It was part of the organization that had always been managed by capable, long-term employees, even before my arrival. Serious or negative issues related to culture or performance were never apparent in that part of the organization, even during the early years of my tenure. It performed well and grew its numbers year over year. A few years after I joined the organization, the long-term head of the eye bank took a different role in the organization. I supported the promotion of a technician to manager to run the eye bank, and it began to return even higher donations than before!

Periodically the Eye Bank Association of America (EBAA), the accrediting body that oversees eye bank procedures, would cite opportunities for improvement from a regulatory point of view, but nothing serious enough to impede its overall success.

Or so we thought.

It turns out the manager who improved the eye bank's productivity numbers had done so at the expense of quality. We had repeatedly talked to him about his disinclination to engage with our expertly trained and nationally recognized VP of quality and regulatory affairs named Jackie Warn, who runs our quality assurance and performance improvement (QAPI) program. The defiant manager felt the numbers he was reporting were good enough that he didn't need to focus his efforts on quality. After he repeatedly failed to follow through on implementing superior quality initiatives, we exited him from the organization.

Our VP of quality met with the eye bank team to go over his departure and hear what they thought was needed from a new eye bank leader to ensure ongoing success. She discovered that one direct report had repeatedly raised concerns to the manager about some of the eye bank practices, and he had shut this person down. That staffer didn't feel they could bring their concerns to anyone else in the organization.

This was a huge miss.

Evidently, the manager had fostered an internal culture in the eye bank where sharing concerns beyond the eye bank was not productive and not appropriate. In retrospect, this stark difference between what was practiced everywhere else in the organization was a blind spot hiding in plain sight. It showed us that our corporate compliance reporting systems had failed if people felt they couldn't speak up with concerns, regardless of their department.

The VP of quality and regulatory affairs immediately brought the issue to me. The senior leadership team then got together to discuss the implications of the documentation gaps to patient safety. These gaps were severe, embarrassing, shameful, and regrettable.

The manager had ordered his staff to skip certain best practice procedures common in the eye banking community. This was a terrible practice that could easily compromise heroic donor eye tissues. It meant healthy and precious eye tissue could be rendered useless.

And in Las Vegas, we were especially aware of the risks of not following proper procedures and staff not speaking up about concerns when standard process is not followed in the extreme case—a local endoscopy and colonoscopy center had infected their patients with hepatitis C and HIV as a result of reusing instruments on live patients in the interest of profit. People lost their medical licenses and were sent to jail.

We were *extremely* lucky that there was no impact to patients and their safety as a result of our non-compliant culture in the eye bank.

That could have given us an out. We could have self-reported a major mistake but stressed that there had been no impact to patient safety.

> BUT WE KNEW WHAT THE RIGHT THING TO DO WAS. AND WE KNEW DOING IT WAS GOING TO BE PAINFUL AS HELL.

That would have been the easier and far less embarrassing path for us to take.

But we knew what the right thing to do was. And we knew doing it was going to be painful as hell.

We made the incredibly difficult decision to immediately halt eye bank operations so as not to continue compromising patient safety. The implications of stopping our efforts meant an indefinite delay in restoring sight from our eye bank all over the world to those in need, which was awful to contemplate. But we needed to address anything that could potentially impact patient safety. I immediately reached out to a trusted colleague and friend from my days at the University of Miami, Elizabeth, who is the longtime executive director of the Florida Lions Eye Bank, which is a world-renowned subdivision of the University of Miami. I uncomfortably included her in our serious plight, and it was the best decision we made. Under the leadership of Jackie and Elizabeth, our teams quickly partnered to foster a very collaborative and value-added rebuilding of our eye bank.

This was a humbling moment for me. This happened on my watch. It felt like I'd let my NDN family, the board, and the people we serve down—much like the feeling I had when my failed invest-ment decisions impacted my family. I felt I had to own it. During a meeting with the board shortly after we uncovered these issues, I went through the painful process of disclosing the details we knew at the time. I also indicated to the board whatever consequences they felt were appropriate for me based on these events, I would fully accept. In the meantime, I would remain focused on being trans-parent and uncomfortably inclusive and ensure this never happened again if given the opportunity to continue as part of the NDN.

We were transparent and held ourselves accountable to all relevant stakeholders and agencies, sharing that we had halted our eye bank operation until we could repair the process in accordance with quality principles led by Jackie and the team. After reporting the issues, we were immediately visited by EBAA auditors and stripped of our accreditation. We also had to report our errors to the FDA, who advised us to issue a recall of all eye tissue we had distributed, which we did. (The FDA isn't heavily involved in organ donation but heavily regulates tissue processing, which includes eye bank tissues.)

Once again, the NDN was back in rarified company: only three eye banks ever (there are approximately seventy-five in the EBAA) had lost their accreditation.

All this played out in the press. We were deeply embarrassed. We were the local press darling for years before this happened, thanks to our transformative success story and growth. This was a *huge* black eye.

We stayed steady and true to our commitment to transparency, uncomfortable inclusion, vulnerability, and accountability. After notifying the board, we commissioned independent third-party audits of all clinical operations to ensure the lack-of-quality dynamic was not pervasive throughout the organization. We reached out to experts and hired objective evaluators who immediately came to the NDN and explored every facet of our operation, and we held nothing back. We did all this within ninety days of uncovering the issues in the eye bank.

Not one of the independent auditors found evidence that the quality adherence, documentation, or fear of reporting issues existed anywhere else within the NDN. Most importantly, we were able to confirm the eye bank issues hadn't directly impacted the safety of any patients.

Three months after we first self-reported and embarked on our CAP, the EBAA restored our eye bank accreditation, the FDA gave us their approval, and we got back to work. The chair of the board, Todd Sklamberg, and members of the NDN board graciously acknowledged that, although this was an egregious error by the organization under my leadership, our decisive, transparent, and inclusive response was to be commended. Todd is a high-performing executive leader and longtime CEO of Sunrise Hospital and Medical Center, which is the largest hospital in Nevada, who I consider a mentor and trusted advisor. I was prepared for whatever consequences they deemed fit, but I am grateful Todd and the board acknowledged and rewarded our true north above all else.

We were clear sighted on what we needed to do moving forward.

INVESTING IN SUCCESS

Over the years, we've iterated the best ways for us to accomplish understanding, participation, and success within the organization. As covered in the previous chapter, every department head gets input from their entire team on SWOT documents and the strategic plan. Everyone participates in designing and implementing success plans based on the goals and tactics each team collectively determines is doable.

We've invested in technology that allows us to input and review data and performance metrics to inform decision-making. Each year, we establish stretch goals, consistently measure how we are tracking against those goals, and course-correct based on what the numbers show us.

When the next year's planning comes around, we create a new goal that will stretch the team's ability to achieve.

I continue to provide the management team with useful business books and tools amassed over my career. We have an ad hoc internal MBA program taking place alongside our ongoing culture initiatives. Any employee who wants to attain an additional academic degree or certifications gets a base sum contributed by the NDN for their tuition. In addition, we have an emerging leaders program that selects high-performing candidates for more substantial tuition reimbursements.

Over time, we have expanded our resources and programs to support the 145 employees working at the NDN. We constantly deploy resources to promote employee well-being, healthy team dynamics, and thriving company culture.

We've got a pretty good process going today, but I imagine we've got another five years of going through an iterative process. That's because the environment changes as we increase our value to and influence on the worldwide organ, tissue, and eye community.

But as long as we're true to our culture, people understand and internalize it better because we've had time to practice and refine it. Our culture is still evolving; it's still a work in progress—which is good, because that means we're still iterating, growing, and getting better every day and every year, no matter what obstacles and challenges we are confronted with.

CHAPTER 8

CULTURE FIRST

The NDN's transformation and yearly record-setting results mean I receive speaking invitations from all over the world. In addition to talking to OPO and tissue organizations worldwide, I've also led discussions about the NDN's turnaround as part of the University of Miami's MBA program, as I shared earlier.

One area of interest is our laser focus on culture and the extensive management resources we utilized to help define and propagate our culture. I always note that culture is the common denominator of all our successes and failures. A robust culture is a multiplier of excellent results (the reverse is also true). Whenever I'm invited to talk about our results, I make it clear that superlative results are contingent on culture.

Nonprofits traditionally haven't been exposed to or engaged with management training resources prevalent in the private industry. When I present, I show the inextricable link between our codified best practices, strong encouragement of accountability, and fostering of an entrepreneurial mindset of "anything is possible," as drivers of our results and increased value to beneficiaries and our partners in the healthcare industry. We are also ultracompetitive, which is a critical component of our success. A competitive nature in the private for-profit world is essential for success but is less prevalent in the nonprofit space, given our survival isn't always tied to our results. At the NDN we want to perform better than any other OPO, save and improve as many lives as possible, and honor the maximum number of donors on behalf of the more than 110,000 men, women, and children who desperately wait for a second chance at life through organ donation and thousands more through tissue and eye donation.

The details and data regarding organ, eye, and tissue procurement and transplantation are fascinating and humbling. For those who are interested, they're included in the appendix section.

Data to measure the effectiveness of OPOs is highly debated and subject to different interpretations based on some complex metrics. One thing is certain: organ donors per million of population and organs transplanted per million of population covered by the OPO *is*

OUR FIELD AND MISSION IS ABOUT HONORING AS MANY DONORS AS WE CAN WHILE TRANSPLANTING AS MANY ORGANS AND TISSUES AS WE CAN FROM EACH DONOR.

very simple to understand, easy to get behind, and is the only internationally recognized metric. We are the best at this metric for many reasons. Remember that psychology exam I aced during my conceptual transformation as a student in college? Well, one of the concepts I studied for that class was Occam's razor, also known as the law of parsimony, a decision-making philosophy in psychology that emphasizes the rationality of simple explanations. If a problem has two possible explanations—a simple one and a complex one, as in the contemplation of OPO metrics—Occam's razor rationalizes that the simple explanation is more likely correct. We believe that if we can be the absolute best at the most simple all-encompassing metric compared to other OPOs all over the world, we will be the absolute best at all other subordinate metrics no matter how far you drill down into complexity. Consequently, if you apply our data to all other outcomes contemplated by our industry, we are also the leaders. Our field and mission is about honoring as many donors as we can while transplanting as many organs and tissues as we can from each potential donor. Being the best on the planet at organ and tissue donors per million of population served and organ and tissues transplanted per million of population served, in my view, takes care of all other metrics if we do it relentlessly and beyond reproach thanks to our high-performing team.

It's true that the NDN's accomplishments since the start of our transformation are impressive. The data on the slides below beautifully illustrate the NDN's transformation from an OPO on the brink of dissolution to one of the world's most productive OPO entities.

Our organization's superlative growth and results did not come from a linear trajectory; there were numerous hiccups and significant setbacks. There were several times when unaddressed undercurrents tugged us off course from our true north.

NEVADA DONOR NETWORK NUMBERS 2011–2019

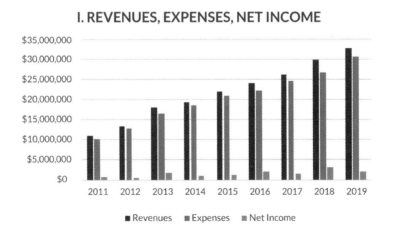

I. REVENUES, EXPENSES, NET INCOME

II. ORGAN DONORS

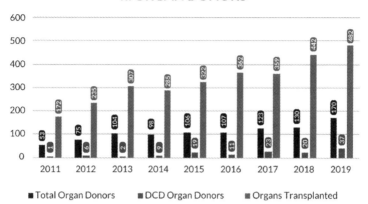

■ Total Organ Donors   ■ DCD Organ Donors   ■ Organs Transplanted

III. TISSUE & EYE DONORS

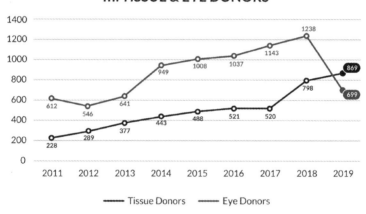

━━ Tissue Donors   ━━ Eye Donors

IV. ORGANS TRANSPLANTED

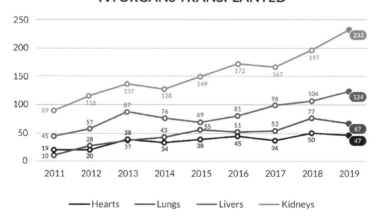

━━ Hearts   ━━ Lungs   ━━ Livers   ━━ Kidneys

V. NUMBER OF DONORS

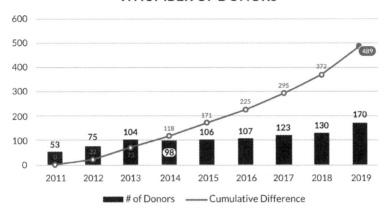

# of Donors   Cumulative Difference

VI. NUMBER OF TRANSPLANTED ORGANS

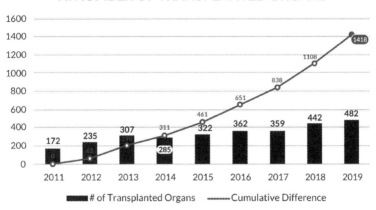

# of Transplanted Organs   Cumulative Difference

VII. NUMBER OF TISSUE DONORS

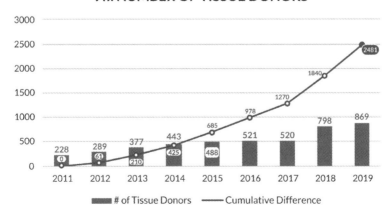

# of Tissue Donors   Cumulative Difference

133

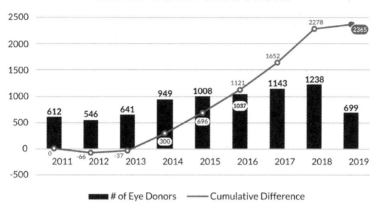

The global benchmark metric is the number of organ donors and transplanted organs per million of population served. This isn't a one-to-one metric, as an individual heroic donor can contribute up to nine lifesaving organs if the liver is split for two patients. Through tissue donation the number can be more than seventy-five life-altering gifts from one heroic donor. We're able to provide corneas to restore sight, skin grafts to burn victims, connective tissue, heart valves, bone grafts, stem cells to research labs, and other applications through the contributions of gifts that can change, extend, and ultimately improve their lives.

All told, our team has facilitated thousands of additional life years to organ recipients who would otherwise have passed away and many more quality years of life to tissue and cornea recipients all over the world because of our transformation.

SUCCESS IS NOT A STRAIGHT LINE

Our data paints a clear story of success. However, successes often come at the expense of mistakes or even flat-out failures. We were not immune to this phenomenon, although the solution was clear from the very beginning.

You've seen a chart like this before:

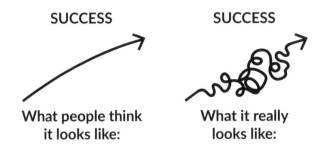

SUCCESS   SUCCESS

What people think   What it really
it looks like: looks like:

If there is one single lesson that any prospective leader or change agent (and anyone can be a change agent) should take away from this book, it is the point illustrated by the chart above.

Success is achievable, even from the bleakest and most dysfunctional starting points.

And success is never linear. It requires hard work, perseverance, and the investment of time. To make a meaningful difference, there must be loyalty to culture by a company's leaders, for a significant amount of time. Turnarounds often happen in organizations, but their efficacy might dwindle as time goes on because leaders move on or lose focus. For sustainable changes, you must put in the time to make the maximum difference and ensure consistency of culture and operations even after a leader departs. Our results are sustainable because people in the organization embrace our culture and carry its message forward to those who join us later. If a leader wants to leave a legacy beyond his or her tenure, longevity of service and loyalty are essential.

SUCCESS IS ACHIEVABLE, EVEN FROM THE BLEAKEST AND MOST DYSFUNCTIONAL STARTING POINTS.

Today, more management resources—informed by successful companies in the private sector—stress the value of learning to recognize failures in a way that doesn't elicit paralyzing emotions, such as fear, shame, and anger. Productively recognizing failure makes practicing accountability a collective cultural imperative. Open dialogue about why something happened rather than blaming someone for a mistake refocuses energies on resolving the process— not the person—that enabled the error.

GROWTH AND ERRORS

Each time the NDN experienced a growth spurt, the organization would regress a little. It's worth digging into the consistent factors of this phenomenon, because the team and I experienced it multiple times.

The NDN had turned itself around operationally during the time described in chapter 5 ("Triage"). The rigorous corrective action plans (CAPs) we put into place worked, generating impressive results.

Our major mistake was in the mindset of focusing exclusively on improving operations in the pursuit of ever-improving results. What we should have been focused on and devoting resources and time to was, of course, our culture.

Remember the first executive survey I conducted when I joined the NDN in 2012? It clearly showed the common denominator of all of the organization's successes and failures—its culture. We had even highlighted culture as *the* main factor upon which our success depended during our presentation to the MPSC.

Then, hooked by our initial success with our CAPs, we doubled down, infusing resources into getting results rather than investing in culture first.

Disregarding the human resources aspect was an understandable mistake, but a mistake nonetheless. During the initial phase of our transformation, I hadn't focused on human resources because we couldn't—we had to immediately focus on improving operational performance to secure approval to keep functioning.

Hiring the NDN ship's crew is one area where this error cost us a lot, more than once. After our first year of success, we had a much larger pool of potential employees from the OPO industry, and I went fishing with a vengeance. We were moving quickly and needed to hire a lot more people. I had my ego and experience whispering in my ear that I knew best about whom to hire.

Of course, I was wrong, as I related earlier in the book. I was noninclusive and hired people based on their paper fit (their résumés and credentials), not their personalities. This was a major error, because no matter how competent a person is, if they don't fit in with an organization culturally, they won't work out. I had to exit every single original new hire I made early on.

Errors happen when you grow quickly. The key is to experience those errors, talk about them openly, do a root-cause analysis, figure out why it happened, and implement measures immediately to prevent it from happening again. And then eventually refine process and procedures so that you can avoid similar errors altogether. We had started to cultivate this cultural openness of admitting fault and error early on in pursuit of operational excellence, but hadn't established it as thoroughly as we thought, as evidenced by the eye bank issue in 2019.

CULTURE FIT

Establishing AQE as our company culture was a top-down decision. I mandated it as our guiding philosophy and core values as soon as I walked in the door. That wasn't particularly collaborative, but it also wasn't a mistake.

When I came on board, the NDN was in complete meltdown.

The team needed me to step in and say, "These values are the ones we are adhering to, starting right now." While we were fighting for survival, we didn't devote time or resources to developing our culture. We had to put everything we had into fixing our operations, and we did.

However, in addition to establishing AQE as our guiding philosophy and core values, I spent time making sure everyone understood AQE was a team process. It didn't work if only a few people adopted AQE as guidelines. Involving teams in explaining and being responsible for AQE was new. I encouraged the senior management team to study those values, engage their teams in discussions of what each value meant, and brainstorm ways to adhere to them. That process was collaborative.

So the AQE values became our strategic anchors keeping us in place. Anchors keep you stabilized, but they don't let you move forward. AQE gave people something to hold on to when they needed it. We invested significant resources around those core values, such as an expensive quality management system, and making self-reporting and accountability core components of our culture.

We eventually built up enough internal muscle to consider our own unique cultural true north rather than borrowing a generic one. Make no mistake: AQE was a critical supporting function in getting the NDN to right itself. AQE should be the baseline for any successful organization. But once AQE became part of our DNA, we needed to create a cultural framework specific to our overall mission. We had to establish a work environment that would empower us to achieve that mission organically.

COLLABORATIVE CULTURE BUILDING

Utilizing common private sector resources came in very useful. AQE had served its purpose. Now we had to build something together from the bottom up, something organic that represented input from the entire organization.

Early on in the NDN's evolution, we worked with The Studer Group, an organization I had worked with at the University of Miami's OPO. The Studer Group, a management training framework for large corporations, is built on the principles outlined in the book *Hardwiring Excellence*.

During one of The Studer Group sessions, the senior management team participated in an exercise about the "Five Dysfunctions of a Team." That's the name of one of the many popular business management books authored by Patrick Lencioni, who also founded The Table Group.

The Five Dysfunctions of a Team—all superprevalent at the NDN—are presented in a pyramid:

Note that results are the last thing on the pyramid. If you rewrite the pyramid more positively, you see all the foundation required to support results. We didn't build this model perfectly the first time. We flipped the pyramid, precariously balancing the organization on results.

A FIRM FOUNDATION

A PRECARIOUS FOUNDATION

After our initial successes in improving our operations and results, we should have taken a big step back and focused on making the NDN a culture-first organization. We knew that culture was the common denominator of all positive and negative occurrences in the company. But we were too enamored with our ongoing improving results. Those results kept us from focusing heavily on culture. After all, we were getting great results just by improving operational efficiency. I know now, and wish I had known then, that our results could have been even more significant if we had invested more strongly in culture first.

The kidney mix-up disaster drove home the importance of addressing culture. In 2015 we engaged The Table Group, Patrick Lencioni's organization. Consultant Michael Lorsch had proactively reached out to us because he had heard how well we were doing after coming out of a very rough spot. He shared that he had worked with OPOs before and thought we'd benefit from investing in a company-strengthening program with The Table Group. His timing was perfect!

Engaging with Michael at The Table Group wasn't an automatic decision. They represented a costly investment in terms of time, funds, and willingness from our management team (and ultimately all employees at the NDN).

It was some of the best money we ever spent.

Under Michael's expert guidance, we slowly recognized how a healthy organization (one with a sustainable and supportive culture) exponentially increases results. Focusing on results first enables blind spots where errors, issues, and adverse events occur; however, the healthy aspects of a culture can be a multiplier of those results, as we learned from Michael based on Lencioni's teachings.

We had multiple management retreats during our freshman

phase, which I facilitated much like I did in my University of Miami OPO days. (I think of our initial year as the freshman year, the few years after as our sophomore year, and now I believe we are at the end of our junior phase/year as an organization.)

During our sophomore years, after each session with Michael, we would go back to the organization, present a condensed form of our goals and discussions, and ask for company-wide feedback. Then we'd go on another management retreat with Michael. Our conversations and debates were sometimes difficult. But we did it as a team—first as a management team and then as an organizational team, when I shared our thoughts in regard to establishing a company culture with the whole organization. Michael artistically helped us process and reflect our collective thoughts in a framework that enabled us to cogently define our organization's core purpose, core values, and strategic anchors.

TOGETHER, THE ORGANIZATION DEFINED WHY WE EXIST: TO PROVIDE *HOPE*, *STRENGTH*, AND *LIFE*.

We didn't pull our culture out of a book. We used a proven process to design our own unique culture and inspiring core values.

Together, the organization defined why we exist: to provide *hope*, *strength*, and *life*.

Those three words became part of our logo.

HOPE	STRENGTH	LIFE
Thousands who await a lifesaving or healing gift have *hope*, thanks to the heroic donors who have given the gifts of life and health.	Donor families who graciously grant the gifts of life and health gain *strength*, knowing they are helping those who may be suffering physically and emotionally while waiting for a second chance.	New *life* is granted to thousands who desperately wait for a transplant thanks to the courageous donors and donor families who gave the ultimate gift.

Through a similar exercise, we defined the NDN's core values as *passion*, *spirit*, and *respect*. Michael masterfully took us through an exercise whereby we identified five of the highest-performing employees on the team and narrowed down the three most common traits they shared to make them the best and what we wanted to replicate in others. We agreed these attributes were mission-critical to our individual and organizational success as a group.

PASSION	SPIRIT	RESPECT
• Expect and celebrate hard work. • Be relentless in your pursuit of *excellence*. • Have the courage to speak up and share ideas. • Show dedication to our organization, mission, and values. • Exude the importance of our mission, and be a champion for donation.	• Work is better when you're having fun. • Encourage positivity despite obstacles; be solution focused. • Show pride in working at NDN. • Celebrate the good; be quick to recognize successes and reward accomplishments. • Be engaged, and get out of your comfort zone. • Embrace *innovation* and *change*; seek out new experiences. • Be *authentic*; embrace *transparency*.	• Be professional in your interactions. • Demonstrate mutual respect for others. • Be *inclusive* and *collaborative*, despite differences and barriers. • Be *accountable* for your actions and to each other. • Actively listen and seek to understand other points of view. • Have reverence for the donors and their families.

Today, each new hire at the NDN has a thirty-minute meeting with me shortly after they join. Sometimes I wear a nutty wig, obnoxious tie, or outsized silly glasses (or all three!). I'm goofy on purpose to show we don't take ourselves too seriously as individuals (which can impede openness and willingness to try new ways of thinking), despite the seriousness of our purpose and function. I don't want new hires to think of the executive team and me as suits. I sit down and tell them about our core purposes of *hope*, *strength*, and *life* and go over our core values of *passion*, *spirit*, and *respect*. I share how we developed those values and what working according to those values looks like at the NDN.

Our core values are a recipe for success at the NDN. Each employee walks away knowing the playbook to follow to thrive and succeed at the NDN and as part of the overall OPO industry. All they have to do is let those concepts guide them.

I talk about how we're serious about our values, and we hold people accountable. It isn't enough to be technically competent; each member of our organization, regardless of title, role, or results, must adhere to our values. Technically superior folks who don't actively respect other people or perspectives get coaching to help them develop that skill, or they are asked to leave if they are unwilling.

Our strategic anchors are *ambition, fun culture,* and *quality. Ambition* because we want to beat the best by a wide margin and then some. *Fun culture* because we spend a lot of time together kicking ass, so we might as well have a fun time doing it. Accountability and excellence are natural supporting attributes to our final strategic anchor of *quality.* If you always strive to perform at the highest levels of quality, you're naturally engaged in the practices of accountability and excellence.

It took us three years to take the time to focus on our culture. We should have done it sooner, once we addressed the immediate threat to our existence.

In the initial management survey and our subsequent seminal presentation to the MPSC, it was clear that culture is the common denominator to *everything* that happens within a company. The entire management team, including me, had to learn this lesson more than once, that the culture we practiced informed our successes. And our failures.

SILVER LININGS

It would have been far better to avoid moments of regression. But even those provided value. Each adverse event forced us to consider a different approach and realize we had to focus more on the organization's culture than on breaking records.

Our openness in sharing our errors, learnings, and CAPs helped engender the support of people in our industry. This was "uncomfortable inclusion" at its finest! We welcomed peer review groups (even critics) and took their feedback seriously. In return, the industry was rooting for us to succeed. It was like the OPO industry and the community as a whole was wrapping their arms around us, saying, "You guys are on the right track, you're doing good things— keep reporting, keep improving, and we think you're going to be a great organization; you just need to grow a little bit." That reinforcement—focusing on what was achievable, rather than the errors—was a crucial stepping-stone that helped us grow into the organization we are today and will be tomorrow.

We maintain our commitment to quality and excellence, and we are supremely, publicly accountable when we fail. Our willingness to share our mistakes and fixes inspires us to new levels of care and efficiency and rewards our industry's faith in our commitment to our mission.

CULTURE GROWTH

Once we finally started focusing on culture first, we evaluated our culture and behavior instead of focusing solely on operational excellence. It became crystal clear that hiring people based on their cultural fit was paramount to operational success. What was equally clear was that I should not be making hiring decisions without input.

Since 2011 the NDN has tripled its number of employees. We've created a Division of Culture, a team of high-performing employees who meet with all potential hires, regardless of seniority or role, to determine a cultural fit. Since we've begun using the Division of Culture as a core component of our hiring process, our recruiting process has improved tremendously. When we hire someone, they are almost always the right fit for our organization.

When people leave the NDN, it's usually for a higher-level role with greater responsibilities at another OPO. Working at NDN is becoming a rite of passage for individuals in the OPO space. Other OPOs often recruit leaders from the NDN because of their experience in our high-performing organization.

INTERNAL INCLUSIVITY

Inclusivity is an essential aspect of our internal promotion and responsibility process. And thank God, because once again, by thinking I knew best and not being inclusive, I almost lost one of our organization's strongest employees and a great leader. Thank goodness we had an established inclusivity platform that forced me to consider input from the team rather than make a call on my own about promoting him.

Here's what happened: We had an effective operational VP of clinical affairs in place who had been doing a good job for a couple of years. Then he got the opportunity to join an OPO in Ohio near his hometown, where he had family to help him and his wife with their new baby. I offered him the COO role at the NDN, a position with significant responsibility given the breadth of our operations, in an effort to keep him. But I couldn't compete with family (or free babysitting)!

During his tenure we were considering the promotion of one of the strongest managers, named Darren, in that department to director, a move I was hesitant to approve. The manager had reported to the prior VP, and he advocated strongly to promote Darren; I didn't personally know how strong his management skills were.

However, the executive team and other members who had worked with Darren strongly supported his promotion to director, against my insular concerns (based mainly on the facts that I hadn't worked directly with him and he hadn't been with the organization long). Later on, I admitted that I felt he needed more time as a manager mainly because I had spent more time in similar roles. The executive team pointed out that my path wasn't the only path to excellence and that it was egotistical and narrow minded for me to think it was.

Thanks to our collaborative and inclusive practices, I backed off from insisting on my narrow and uninformed point of view, and we promoted Darren to director. He immediately began improving processes to the point where the results from his department were higher than ever. He got rave reviews from his peers and team members. Fast-forward to his supervisor leaving in 2019 for free babysitting, and I was championing promoting him to VP to succeed the departing VP. Now I know that when people you trust identify someone as the right person to take on more responsibility, you should back that person 100 percent. I did, and now we're positioning this guy to be our next COO.

Thank God for our culture of respect, inclusivity, and collaboration. Without it, I probably would have just followed my contrary instincts, wasted time, annoyed the executive team, and lost an excellent colleague.

ONWARD AND UPWARD

As you can see from the story above, culture helps you stay on course in your pursuit of true north.

Our focus on culture first is why—eight years into our transformation—we perform at a higher level than before, with more stability and reliability.

It has been an uncomfortable, complicated, and messy process along the way. It was never a straight line. But we kept chipping away and relying on best practices to keep us strategically anchored and on our true north path. The answer was in plain sight from day one. I am sure we will experience raging currents and weather as we continue our journey.

FOCUSING ON CULTURE FIRST IS PARAMOUNT TO A HEALTHY AND PRODUCTIVE WORKPLACE.

Multiple adverse events reminded us that focusing on culture first is paramount to a healthy and productive workplace.

Today we continue to outperform the records we established the year before thanks to our amazing team, the heroic donors, and courageous families. We continue to think about more ways to provide value to our partners in the healthcare ecosystem to promote hope, strength, and life in the United States and worldwide. As such, we follow and measure international metrics while actively engaging with the international community every chance we get. This practice of international inclusion was instilled in me by my parents raising us to encourage diversity and inclusion and from the widespread international ties I forged in Miami at the University of Miami OPO.

NDN is a member of the International Society of Organ Donation and Procurement (ISODP), which holds a convention every two years. I've attended its meetings in Sydney, Australia; Geneva, Switzerland; and Dubai, United Arab Emirates.

In 2021 the ISODP convention is scheduled to take place in Las Vegas, United States. The NDN is the lead organizer, and I'll be cochairing the event with the president and council of the ISODP.

We'll have plenty of sessions about best practices. We'll share examples of our expanded relationships with local stakeholders who help us fulfill our mission better and whom we support in return. We'll talk about our entrepreneurial mindset and how it led to creating a new type of international joint venture that helps facilitate tissue donation and transplantation in other countries. At the same time, and above all else, we will highlight our cultural framework in which these best practices are implemented as the most important factor in our success.

Our entire goal is to share our stories—warts and all—behind our cultural best practices with the global community to increase the efficiency and productivity of OPOs worldwide.

In short, we'll be focusing on transplanting success through uncomfortable inclusion.

AFTERWORD

Uncomfortable Inclusion is a book about business, with a few personal life learnings along the way. There's one more story, still unfolding, where my personal and professional achievements are deeply intertwined.

In 2016 I thought I had reached a pinnacle in my life by achieving my MBA, getting the job of my dreams, and leading a dramatic transformation at the NDN. I was a forty-one-year-old bachelor with a fantastic job, an amazing team, and a supportive family, and I was traveling all over the world, telling the story of NDN. What could be better?

I was having a great time enjoying what felt like a blessed existence.

I had no idea I was about to experience similarly seismic events in my personal life.

One rare July weekend night, I was home in Las Vegas rather than out traveling. The advent of Zappos and its employees had transformed downtown Las Vegas; there was always a busy local social scene. I decided on a whim to go out and treat myself to a drink at the Commonwealth, a speakeasy bar that is known for its excellent drinks, food, and old-school dance music.

I was just expecting a fun evening of casual conversation.

* * *

Sasha has piercing green eyes, a stunning smile, and an incredible personality. That night she was celebrating completing her medical school exams and was looking to blow off some steam.

We began talking and didn't stop until 4:00 a.m. To this day I don't know how I worked up the courage to ask if I could buy her a drink. We had one of those insanely vulnerable conversations that leave you feeling shaken afterward. We shared and discussed everything.

Born in Russia, Sasha had lived in the United States since she was fifteen, away from her parents and sister for most of her life. She was awarded a prestigious scholarship through an exchange program, thanks to her excellent grades and amazing talents. I had blown off most of my educational career and spent most of my life surrounded by family. She was a Russian Jew; I was a Brazilian Catholic. We were total opposites.

Sasha had completed her undergraduate degree in Flint, Michigan (the same state where my father had finalized his medical training) before coming to Las Vegas to attend medical school.

We were dizzy thinking about the scenarios that had occurred all over the world that ended up with the two of us at a bar that night in Las Vegas: Yekaterinburg, Russia; Flint, Michigan; New Haven, Connecticut; Alice, Texas; Miami, Florida; Januária, Brazil; and then … finally, Las Vegas, Nevada!

We began dating right away. For one of our first vacations together, I wanted to take Sasha to Atlantis in Nassau, the Bahamas, one of my favorite places in the world. To get there, we had to spend a night in Miami at the Biltmore Hotel, which was cool, as I wanted to show her some of my favorite places there. I booked a single night in Miami. Sasha was perplexed, as she knew how close I was to my family. And she knew I was wild about her. So why weren't we going to spend time with my family?

Because I had never talked about my personal life with my family. I just didn't.

Until Sasha.

I had to have some fun with it. I first told my mom I met a cool dancer at a bar in Las Vegas, and I was bringing her home to meet the family. Sasha *is* an experienced ballroom dancer. I held out as long as I could, listening to my mother trying to suppress her concern before I broke down laughing and shared that Sasha was an aspiring neurologist who just happened to dance socially.

The first night Sasha and I arrived in Miami, we all had dinner with my family at a Brazilian steakhouse called Texas De Brazil in South Beach. It was love at first sight. Sasha and my father spent the night trading doctor war stories. My father had been a medical resident in Detroit, Michigan, at Henry Ford Hospital, in a community where Sasha had spent some time working and would be interviewing for a residency spot.

The doctors who interviewed Sasha at the residency program at the Las Vegas hospital noted that her board scores meant she could go to more prestigious programs. They wanted to know why she wanted to stay in Las Vegas to train at the smaller two-resident program. She truthfully said that if she went to a large program, she would get lost in a sea of colleagues, whereas if she stayed in Las Vegas, she'd get to do more and get more training. Given the shortage of doctors in Nevada, residents get to do more actual "doctoring" when they are in training.

Sasha ranked Valley Hospital in Las Vegas as her number one choice during the residency match process, and they ranked her as their number one choice, so she was able to stay in Las Vegas. Whew!

By 2017 we were living together, and I was thinking about how I wanted to propose to this amazing woman. I didn't know anything other than I wanted it to be *epic*.

In the spirit of inclusivity, I began sourcing ideas from my friends and family. First, I reached out to Larry Barnard, the CEO of a major local hospital system in Las Vegas. He is also a member of our advisory board at NDN. This guy is one of the most creative people I know. He's a great friend and successful hospital CEO who went to West Point and became a helicopter pilot for the army, and he has a beautiful family.

I told Larry about how soccer (or, more accurately, *futebol*) is life in Brazil. My siblings and I are obsessed, and we grew up cheering for Brazil (and the US soccer team, of course). In 2014 my entire family went to Brazil when that country hosted the World Cup.

When Russia announced it would be hosting the World Cup in 2018, I realized I could combine soccer with asking my soul mate to marry me. And one of the games would be played in Sasha's hometown, Yekaterinburg, Russia. That was it. I decided that's where I would propose *if* we were lucky enough to score tickets to that game!

A lottery system determines the tickets for World Cup games, which added an element of uncertainty to my proposal plan. Using our respective Russian and Brazilian passports (both Sasha and I have dual citizenship), we selected the games we wanted to attend. Sasha scored tickets to all four games we wanted in Moscow, St. Petersburg, Kazan, and Yekaterinburg!

Larry suggested I find out where Sasha's father had proposed to her mother and propose to Sasha in the same place. I thought that was a *great* idea. I loved Sasha's parents, whom I'd met when they had visited Las Vegas to celebrate her graduation from medical school.

Unfortunately, they didn't speak much English, and I knew almost no Russian. Sasha was our ever-present translator, but obviously, I couldn't use her for this mission.

While I was figuring out how to talk to Sasha's father, Larry upped the ante, suggesting I invite my entire family to Russia for the

World Cup to be present when I proposed to Sasha. That certainly would be epic, in both results and logistics. I put that idea on hold until I could figure out how to talk to Sasha's parents.

I turned to Google Translate and Facebook Messenger and sent Sasha's father, Victor, and her mother, Luba, this note:

Victor: I hope you and Luba are doing well. Sasha and I are doing very well. We are especially excited about our upcoming trip to visit you and your family in Russia. I love your daughter more than anything in the Universe, and I am looking forward to visiting your homeland where you and Luba raised her to become the magnificent woman that she is.

Before I tell you the purpose of this note, I want to deeply apologize for not asking this question in person given the distance between us and my inability to speak your language. I hope you will forgive me for the impersonal nature of this communication; especially given the importance of this request and my respect for you.

To that end, I would like to request your permission to ask Sasha to marry me and be my wife. Sasha has told me a great deal about her upbringing and your sacrifices to raise your children in such a profound way. If you grant me this request, I will be profoundly grateful and vow to spend the rest of my life making sure she has the beautiful life she deserves and is always honored the way you would hope and expect for her.

If you will allow me, I plan to propose to her as a surprise during our trip to Russia. I would also like to know precisely where you proposed to Luba as I would like to ask Sasha for her hand in marriage in the same place. If this is possible, I know it will mean a great deal to Sasha and I, as long as she says YES!

Thank you for your consideration of my request. I look forward to receiving your response.
Sincerely,
Joe

I sent the note at 5:30 p.m. Las Vegas time and didn't expect a response until morning. Later that night, I got an answer—the angry-face emoji—which sent me fleeing from the bed into the bathroom with my phone to figure out what horrible translation mistake I made.

To my relief, the error was on Victor's end; he had simply hit the wrong key. We sent laughing emojis back and forth before he and Luba gave me their permission to ask for Sasha's hand in marriage. They shared that it was clear to them how much we loved each other. However, their proposal had taken place in a hostel near a factory where they worked. He wasn't sure if the hostel was still there, and he said the area wasn't particularly romantic or meaningful to Sasha. He still found and sent me pictures of that location, and then he told me about a gorgeous park nearby named after Victor Mayakovsky, a famous Russian poet from the early 1900s. Sasha and her sister used to play in that park as kids. Victor suggested that as a more romantic alternative. I spent some time googling the poet Mayakovsky and found this translated excerpt from a long poem he wrote in 1922:

Outcome:

Neither miles
nor quarrels
can make love perish.
Thought out
and tested
all through.
Raising the sheet of verses,
my cherished,—
I swear that my love is both,
constant and true!

I decided to memorize this part of the poem and weave it into my proposal. Victor was right; the park was a great place to propose to Sasha. Another win for inclusivity and collaboration!

Then I went into full conspiracy planning mode. I talked to Victor every day, putting the plans into place. We booked tickets for planes, trains, and automobiles; reserved hotel rooms; bought more game tickets; and created detailed itineraries for my entire family. It was a wonderful, insane time.

It was also a confusing time for Sasha. She enjoyed a close relationship with my family, engaging in frequent and long conversations with them. Sasha noticed my family was talking to her less, which she found odd. Of course, she didn't realize it was because they were afraid they would say something that would spoil the surprise!

Sasha and I would fly from Las Vegas to New York, then on to London, where we would spend a few days before arriving in Yekaterinburg. The jeweler from whom I bought the engagement ring advised me not to keep it in the box (as it is common for TSA agents to ask people to open jewelry boxes) and certainly not to pack it in my luggage.

I spent a terrifying few days in New York and London, and a few hours in Istanbul, with a diamond ring shoved casually into my jacket pocket.

While Sasha and I were on our way to Russia, my family spent time in Lisbon, Portugal. They were due to arrive in Yekaterinburg the day before we did. The plan was for Victor to pick them up and get them settled. Then he would ferry them to where I planned our proposal.

Of course, when man makes plans, God laughs. In Moscow, my family missed their connection to Yekaterinburg. The next flight to Yekaterinburg landed thirty minutes before ours!

I was alerted to this, but there was nothing I could do. Victor and Luba were on top of all of it—my family would be arriving in Yekaterinburg on a domestic flight from Moscow, and Sasha and I would be arriving on an international flight from Istanbul, so we would be in different terminals.

When my family landed, Victor rushed them through baggage and out the door to their hotel transport, while Luba greeted us outside of customs and dawdled until she got the all-clear from Victor that it was safe to let us proceed.

Larry—my friend with ideas—suggested I hire a "hidden" photographer to follow Sasha and me and take pictures of the proposal. I had no idea how I would begin to go about doing that and asked Victor. Sasha's family saved the day again: her aunt gave us the present of a photo shoot. And the family filled in the photographer on what was *really* happening, so he was aware. This was good, because I still didn't speak Russian, and the photographer didn't speak any English.

On the big day, our photographer, who doubled as our driver, took Sasha and me to the park, where we began to wander around. He looked at me expectantly a few times, but no place clicked. Sasha began to suspect something. As we walked toward a Ferris wheel (the proposal location contender), I saw a gorgeous water fountain and realized that was the perfect place.

We walked toward the fountain and posed for a few photos. I looked at Sasha and committed myself to that moment, and that moment only.

Then I recited the excerpt of the poem I had memorized:

Neither miles nor quarrels can make love perish.
Thought out and tested all through.
Raising the sheet of verses, my cherished,
I swear that my love is both, constant and true!

Sasha's eyes filled with tears as I knelt on one knee and asked her to marry me. She said yes!

We got great pictures.

After a few minutes of laughing and hugs, I said, "I have another surprise for you!" before I realized that I had no idea where our families were! Because I hadn't wanted to be on my phone, I hadn't kept them informed of our precise location. Luckily, they anticipated I'd be distracted and were keeping an eye out. Moments later, a small park tour trolley burst into the clearing, carrying our entire families—grandparents, aunts, parents, siblings, everyone!

Sasha was speechless. It was an awesome, epic moment. She couldn't get over how all of these people had converged in her hometown to celebrate our proposal.

It was an unbelievable, priceless moment that I will never forget.

***

Sasha and I got married in Key Largo, a place we both love, while looking out at the ocean and surrounded by our family and friends. I even invited everyone from the NDN who wanted to attend!

My vow to Sasha delivered in front of our loved ones:

> *My queen, my mermaid, my eternal love and my soul mate. Before I met you, I didn't exist. I was under the illusion that my life was complete. And now, with the privilege and honor of marrying you tonight in front of our loved ones, life has new meaning. My love for you is infinite, which knows no bounds and is beyond measure. I promise and vow to always honor you, respect you, love you, and protect you until my last breath on this earth and throughout eternity in my soul. Although it is impossible to adequately convey my passion, love and commitment to you in words, please know that as God and all of our beloved gathered here today as my witnesses, I vow to provide all that I have in me to make your dreams come true and bring joy to you and our unborn children in a way that you will always cherish for as long as we both shall live and exist in the universe.*

The night before our wedding, the AOPO (Association of Organ Procurement Organizations) selected three new representatives for their executive board. On the day of our wedding, I got a morning phone call letting me know I would be one of those elected representatives the following year. In June 2020, I began my one-year term as the president of the AOPO, a significant honor and professional accomplishment.

All my professional aspirations, all the ups and downs, had led me to Sasha. Because others supported, influenced, and nudged me personally and professionally, I found myself in an even more wonderful place in 2020: welcoming our first child together. I credit most of my successes to getting over myself and letting people in to advise me—even when it was uncomfortable!

When our son (or children) grows up, I look forward to telling him stories like the ones in this book, about stumbling and discovering the right way on this complicated journey called life.

I traveled a very windy, broken road, filled with struggles and challenges. It was an arduous and rewarding process to get to the NDN and Las Vegas, where I got to meet, marry, and start a family with my soul mate.

I never thought my life would be interesting enough to write about. If sharing the outcome of my journey of choices, successes, mistakes, people in my life, signs from the universe, and so on can help one person achieve what they wish for, this book will be worth it.

* * *

Compared to many others around the world, I have not had a rough life. On the contrary, my life has been charmed, thanks to the care and love of many other people. I still found myself in tough spots (many self-imposed), but once I committed to living the lessons I learned (and now teach), it has been mostly smooth sailing.

I will continue to pay attention to the universe and amazing people in my life, because there are still more lessons to be learned.

I learned from wise and knowledgeable people around me to recognize the navigational beacons put out by the universe, while staying bold, being inclusive, taking risks, and following my heart. I'm grateful to everyone who influenced me, taught me, and guided me in both minor and major ways. I am blessed with a magical, wonderful life.

To my readers and my recently born son:

Uncomfortable, unpredictable, and magical events alike will shape your business and personal life. You must seize whatever you are dealt and make the best of it with relentless passion. You must not lose sight of your true north or what you are trying to accomplish.

Whether you are trying to build the best organization in the universe or marrying your soul mate (or both!), stay the course. Don't give up, no matter what.

Eleanor Roosevelt said, "I am who I am today because of the choices I made yesterday."

You must seek out the impossible and persevere through the difficult. Otherwise, you will not achieve the best version of yourself.

Wishing you smooth sailing and following seas.

—Joe Ferreira

ACKNOWLEDGMENTS

To my mermaid and soulmate, Sasha: I am so grateful our paths crossed. Life's meaning became clear when I met you. I love you infinitely.

To our son, Joey: You are destined for greatness. No matter where your individual journey takes you do not let any obstacle, mistake, or challenge define you. Instead, let it propel you higher by focusing on doing the right thing and your true north. I love you, and we are here for you no matter what.

To my brothers and sister: Priscilla, Alex, and Sergio, you are the best siblings I could have asked for. I love you all.

To the team and volunteers at Nevada Donor Network (both past and present): The pride and love I feel to be part of this team and the honor to serve this mission with you is indescribable. Thank you for your passion and for teaching me what it means to serve with a purpose.

To the NDN Governing and Advisory Board Members (both past and present): Thank you for your trust and the opportunity to be a part of such a magical story that is still being told.

To the heroic donors, their courageous families, and the brave transplant recipients: Serving you is the greatest honor of my life. Thank you for representing the absolute best humanity has to offer through organ, eye, and tissue donation for transplantation.

To Les Olson: Thank you for sharing your clinical expertise, friendship, and mentorship when it mattered most.

To Leslie Cortina: Thank you for seeing the potential in me and for not giving up on me.

To the pack of wild transplant surgeons who raised me, including Dr. Levi, Dr. Tzakis, Dr. Burke, Dr. Ciancio, Dr. Moon, Dr. Ricci, Dr. Pham, Dr. Panos, Dr. Miller, Dr. Kado, Dr. Nishida, Dr. Chen, Dr. Selvaggi, Dr. Guerra, Dr. Franco, Dr. Figuero, and Dr. Vianna: Thank you putting up with this crazy kid while molding me to appreciate the art and power of your magical skill of transplantation on behalf of those who desperately wait.

To Aaron Gilchrist: Thank you for connecting the dots to make this book possible. You are a great friend, trusted counselor, and true colleague.

To Carrie Deese: Thank you for supporting me as a friend and colleague during the MBA program and throughout my career. Could not have done it without you all those years.

To Esther-Marie Carmichael: Thank you for your expert guidance and counsel as a friend and colleague. Your role as a quality expert, CMS veteran, and donor family member has been a godsend which I will always be thankful for.

To Deborah Roth: Thank you for helping me capture and memorialize this magical journey through your talent and insight. You have a gift and I am grateful you shared it with me to help tell our priceless story.

To Gian "John" Brown: Thank you for your expert counsel, attentiveness, and friendship on this journey. Your legal and governance knowledge has been key to our success along the way.

To colleagues, partners, and mentors throughout the years: Thank you for your patience, time, and counsel to help me learn, grow, and strive for my full potential even when it was not easy to get through to me.

ORGAN DONATION AND TRANSPLANTATION

This is my overview of how the organ procurement and transplantation process works. If you are interested in this topic and would like additional details, please visit the comprehensive US Department of Health and Human Services website pages at: https://optn.transplant.hrsa.gov/learn/about-donation/ and https://www.organdonor.gov/about/process.html.

There are four stages to the OPO process:

Notification and monitoring—The point when the OPO is notified about an imminent death and/or end-of-life decision (where care is futile).

Evaluation and authorization—What occurs when a person is evaluated to become a heroic donor and authorization is obtained.

Allocation and recovery—The actual process of allocating the organs to the intended recipients and the surgical recovery of the gifts from the donor.

Recipient preparation and transplantation—The final decision by the transplant surgeon and team to implant the organ and prepare the recipient.

NOTIFICATION AND MONITORING

Every hospital in the country is required to have a contractual agreement with its federally designated OPO in the DSA for organ donation. The Nevada Donor Network has contracts with 80 percent of the hospitals in Nevada, and our agreement encompasses the donation of tissues and eyes.

When a person in one of those hospitals is not expected to survive a devastating injury, the hospital notifies the OPO. The potential organ donor notification makes the OPO aware of a mechanically ventilated and critically injured individual with a brain injury who possesses a physical profile that may fit the general criteria for organ, tissue, and eye donation.

Not every notification results in a heroic donor. Many patients referred to the OPO may not meet the criteria for donation, either because they improve or have a clinical issue that makes them ineligible to donate.

We have what we call a Donation Services Center, which is essentially a twenty-four seven call center that receives notifications from hospitals and other community partners such as coroners, medical examiners, law enforcement, funeral homes, and hospice centers for potential tissue and eye donation.

In order to streamline and improve the process, several OPOs like us are participating in the development of an automated referral system from the hospital's electronic medical record for patients meeting referral criteria. Initial results indicate that this process is less strenuous on the hospital staff who are required to call our center and spend time on the phone with our team despite all their other demands. Upon receiving the automated referral, if the circumstances described during the notification suggest a potential donor, the process begins.

EVALUATION AND AUTHORIZATION

The first part of the process is a clinical evaluation. An OPO team member conducts a physical, informational, and clinical assessment of the patient. They determine a patient's physical state and whether or not the family is engaged in the patient's care.

It is the hospital's responsibility to tell a family that their family member is brain dead or that there is no hope for meaningful recovery. There are times when OPO personnel are present or even participate in that conversation as part of end-of-life discussions. In order for a family to contemplate donation, they need to process and understand that their loved one is legally, clinically, and ethically deceased.

We only engage with the family after it is confirmed that there is no hope for a meaningful recovery despite the healthcare team's best efforts. In many cases family members don't want their loved ones to continue with minimal brain function, and they make the difficult decision to remove life support.

The first priority for all donation professionals is the care and comfort of the next of kin and family of the potential donor. Once their emotional needs are met and they express an understanding of their loved one's condition, only then can we have a conversation about the donation option. By that time, the OPO team knows if the person under discussion is registered in the national and statewide database as an organ, tissue, and eye donor. If so, this fact is incorporated into the discussion.

When someone signs up to be an organ donor, that creates a legally binding authorization to proceed with donation once they are deceased. In that case, the OPO is not required to ask the family for permission to authorize the donation process. Generally, those discussions are much less painful and uncertain for the family because they know donation is what their loved one wanted to do. There's no decision for them to make. We disclose to the family that we are going to honor their loved one's wish to be a donor, and that they have the ability to participate in the process, as much or as little as they'd like. An overwhelming majority of the time, families are completely on board with the process of donation. They're relieved that they don't have to make the decision, and they support the process.

If the individual hasn't signed up to be an organ, tissue, or eye donor, then conversations are conducted with their next of kin and family by the OPO team. Even when someone is registered as an organ, tissue, and eye donor, families who are in shock and grieving very rarely may not agree with what their loved one would have wanted. In those rare cases, we work with the family to help them understand the legality of their loved one's wishes to be a donor with great compassion and understanding.

When someone isn't a registered donor, the conversation is different. We gently and compassionately ask the next of kin and family if they want their loved one to leave a legacy as an organ, tissue, and eye donor. If they agree, then the process shifts from the hospital's aegis over to the OPO once they are declared brain dead for organ donation and circulatory death for tissue and eye donation. Depending on the region, the recovery process most often takes place in the hospital operating room (OR) for organ donation. Some OPOs have recovery centers in their facilities that contain ICU-like environments and operating rooms. In order to facilitate tissue and eye donation, this can occur in a special "clean room" at the coroner's office, a funeral home, or at the tissue bank facility.

The doctors and nurses at the hospital are 100 percent focused on saving a person, as a priority. When it is clear that a person cannot be saved, they must move on to help the next person. Once an individual is confirmed as a donor and is declared brain dead or dead by circulatory criteria, OPO personnel take over, and attention focuses on ensuring optimum support for their family, organs, tissues, and eyes.

ALLOCATION AND RECOVERY

We input all relevant donation characteristics, such as lab values and medical and social history, into a national donor medical database called DonorNet, which sends out an electronic bulletin to transplantation centers with candidates waiting on the specific organs the OPO has available to recover. Transplant coordinators and surgeons review individual organs for their candidate.

Notifications are prioritized based on a number of factors, such as how long a prospective recipient has been on a wait list, how sick they are, and their compatibility with the donor. Multiple candidates are notified of a potential donor organ, but they also know where they stand on the list: the primary candidate has first right of refusal. We can notify up to five prospective recipients at a time. Their respective medical teams have an hour to assess and make a decision on whether or not to accept the organ for the primary recipient. But candidates farther down the list are at least alerted to the possibility of a donation and know to stay vigilant to the chance that the initial candidate will turn down the gift, passing that opportunity on to their team to evaluate the organ(s) for them.

Multiple teams get notified for the different organs such as heart, lungs, liver, pancreas, and kidneys. Each transplant center sends a surgeon and team to facilitate the recovery if a local recovery surgeon is not available. Coordinating the different surgical teams is incredibly complicated.

Recovery takes one of two paths, depending on whether an individual experiences brain death or circulatory death. The two paths are Donation after Brain Death (DBD) and Donation after Circulatory Death (DCD). In both types of donors, they must be declared deceased by law and ethical standards before any organs or tissues are recovered. There is an actual law in place to mandate this minimum and necessary condition called the Uniform Determination of Death Act, otherwise known as the "Dead Donor Rule."[6]

DBD occurs after someone suffers a devastating and irreversible brain and brain stem injury that results in the diagnosis of brain death.[7] These potential donors still have a heartbeat and a pulse during the organ recovery process, but they are legally deceased by neurological criteria. After organ donation is completed, tissues and eyes can also be recovered.

DCD occurs when organ donation takes place after someone is declared dead by cardiac and circulatory arrest. These occur when someone suffers a brain injury that is devastating and irreversible, except that the potential donor cannot be declared brain dead by neurological criteria. In these cases, the family elects to withdraw clinical support from their loved one when there is no hope for a meaningful recovery. Once support is withdrawn and the person experiences irreversible cardiac and circulatory arrest, organ recovery takes place. Tissue and eye recovery may be performed after death has been declared and the surgical recovery of organs is completed.

6   A. S. Iltis and M. J. Cherry, "Death Revisited: Rethinking Death and the Dead Donor Rule," *Journal of Medicine and Philosophy* 35(3), 2010, 223–241.

7   Eelco F.M. Wijdicks, MD, PhD, et al., "Evidence-based guideline update: Determining brain death in adults," American Academy of Neurology, accessed September 22, 2020, https://emcrit.org/wp-content/uploads/determining-brain-death.pdf.

Once we have confirmed organ allocation to the accepting centers for specified candidates, we schedule an OR time, and recovery personnel fly in to the OPO's DSA to help with recovery specific to the organ their patient will receive. The hospital provides an anesthesiologist and staff in the OR to support the process and manage the ventilator during the procurement of the organs.

After death is declared by cardiac and circulatory criteria, the procurement team must wait up to five minutes before they may enter the donor's surgical suite to confirm the absence of a heartbeat or a pulse. This is not the case for BD donors because they are legally deceased, despite having a pulse and heartbeat.

Prior to the recovery of organs, there is a moment of silence to honor the donor before the surgery begins. In certain circumstances we also perform what is called an honor walk in the hospital, where doctors and nurses line the halls of the hospital on the way from the ICU to the OR where the surgery will take place. The families of the donor heroes are especially grateful for this because it honors their loved one in their final hours on the way to give the gift of life and health. We regard all donors as heroes and treat their reverent act of giving life and health to others as a sacred process at every step to ensure the family finds comfort in the process and the legacy their loved one left. There are a ton of technical aspects and best practices for what we do. But it is the humanistic and altruistic gift through grief and loss that keeps us going with passion, spirit, and respect! The donors and their families teach us that even when things are at their darkest, there can be hope and strength. They also teach us how fragile life is, and that we should cherish every moment.

Once the hospital physician confirms that there has been no sign of circulation or heartbeat and no autoresuscitation for five minutes, the patient is brought into the OR for donation after circulatory death. The visualization of blood vessels and organ preservation is conducted upon the commencement of the surgical procedure after death has been declared by circulatory criteria. For brain death donation, this process can occur while the heart is still beating, and mechanical support is provided because these donors have been declared dead by neurological criteria.

When a brain-dead patient is in the OR, thoracic surgeons cross-clamp the thoracic aorta, and immediately the preservation solutions are infused and ice is placed in the thoracic cavity and in the abdomen. All blood is flushed out and replaced with the solutions that are specially designed to preserve organs under what's called cold ischemia conditions, which means they're devoid of blood supply and preserved in a cold environment. That means organs go straight from normal oxygenation perfused by blood at body temperature—provided by a heartbeat and normal blood flow—to cold storage, with the goal of reduced cellular metabolism to maintain adequate viability until they can be transplanted.

The organs are placed in insulated packages designed to offer the most protection and labeled with data about the contents within.

RECIPIENT PREPARATION AND TRANSPLANTATION

After the surgical recovery is completed, organs are sent—based on the criticalness of care—via charter jet, courier flights, or regular packaging services, to their intended location.

Based on the immediate need, organs are received and transplanted. Eyes and tissues are processed and placed into a bank for surgeons to utilize as needed.

The complexity of the process by the transplant center is monumental. Careful planning on behalf of the recipients for such a complex procedure requires optimal communication, equipment, and talented personnel to make sure the transplant procedure in the accepting hospital is successful. Once a compatible organ becomes available for a patient, the transplant center staff contacts the potential recipient to give them the life-changing news. This notification is often emotional for the patient and their family due to what it means for them. Unfortunately, far too many people wait for a call that never comes due to the shortage of organs available.

What makes this process so challenging for the transplanting center is the unpredictability of a donor organ becoming available for their patient. Once they are notified, there is a sense of urgency to make travel arrangements, staff a surgical suite, obtain blood products, and prepare specialized equipment—all intense time constraints. The transplant team must often send surgeons and staff to perform the recovery and return to participate in the surgical implantation of the organ. This results in sleep deprivation and the opportunity for a multitude of factors that may render the organ unusable. In some circumstances, a team is dispatched after the patient is notified of an available organ, only to cancel the procedure later if complications arise.

The reality is that our ecosystem and transplantation is based on bringing together the passing of a donor under challenging circumstances with their own medical conditions and social history coupled with a very sick patient suffering from a host of medical conditions and challenges. These circumstances are brought together, and the expectation is that these organs are going to save the patient's life. The pressure on the transplant staff is enormous while they use their best judgment to bring these factors together with a positive outcome.

This is why at the Nevada Donor Network we overaccommodate the needs of the transplant center while honoring the heroic donor, and we work hard to ensure the best outcome of the recipient under these strenuous circumstances. Our role is to maximize the odds that the heroic donor organs and tissues will be accepted and transplanted by the transplanting centers. We work vigorously and passionately on behalf of the heroic donor and their family to make this possible. At the same time, the ultimate decision of whether or not an organ is transplanted rests with the transplant center staff acting on behalf of the patients in desperate need.

HONORING HEROIC DONORS AND DONOR FAMILY CARE

Privacy and confidentiality laws around donations are strict. If a family wants to know, we can tell them their loved one's heart is going to a fifty-five-year-old mother. If the donation is successful and both sides wish it, we facilitate anonymous communication between the donor family and the recipient center. Eventually, if those indirect communications are successful, we may coordinate a meeting between them if ample time has passed as both the donor family and recipient heal.

We continue to provide care and comfort to the donor family in their grieving process even after donation has already taken place. We have a full-time donor family aftercare coordinator. Her entire job is to correspond and work with donor families to get them whatever resources they need to help with their grieving process.

Every OPO has a similar program. The OPO process doesn't stop at the point a family or their loved one made a decision and the recovery process has taken place. We continue to care for and honor heroic donors and their families year over year.

If you're interested in becoming a registered donor, you can do so at www.registerme.org.